Speed Leadership

A New Way to Lead for Rapidly Changing Times

Bob Emiliani, Ph.D.

Foreword by Massimo Torinesi

■ Second Edition ■

The CLBM, LLC
Wethersfield, Conn.

Speed Leadership: A Better Way To Lead In Rapidly Changing Times / M.L. "Bob" Emiliani. Foreword by Massimo Torinesi.

Cover design and illustrations by Bob Emiliani. Illustrations in Foreword by Massimo Torinesi.

ISBN-13: 978-0-9898631-6-2

Library of Congress Control Number: 2015909964

1. Leadership 2. Management 3. Business 4. Organizations

First Edition: July 2015
Second Edition: October 2015

Published previously as an e-book titled: *Nobody Is Exempt From Improvement: How Improving Leadership Processes Improves Leaders' Credibility and Effectiveness* (2013). This print version is revised and expanded.

Published by The CLBM, LLC, Wethersfield, Connecticut, USA

Manufactured using digital print-on-demand technology.

To Lucinda

CONTENTS

Foreword

He that will not apply new remedies must expect new evils; for time is the greatest innovator. - Francis Bacon

Leadership and learning are indispensable to each other.
- John F. Kennedy

*   *   *   *

In a scorched wasteland, by the light of a campfire, a disheveled man tells a group of children a story. In the shadows created by the light of the flames, he explains:

"Yes, the planet got destroyed. But for a beautiful moment
in time we created a lot of value for shareholders."

It was with this cartoon from *The New Yorker* magazine that I began our workshop in Italy for managers and entrepreneurs with Bob Emiliani. The idea I wanted to express, with force and incisiveness, is that we cannot condone everything, that the end does not justify the means, and that leaders are duty bound to define the "ends" worth persevering for.

In these unsettled times, a serious lack of leadership is detectable across the board; from politics (in Europe an incapacity of vision has been made apparent by the handling of the Greek crisis and immigration problem) to the subject matter of this book, organizations and businesses.

What you are about to begin reading is not a typical management book, but an immense distillation of ideas on leadership from a unique perspective, packed with stimuli.

According to 2013 Gallup research (*State of the Global Workplace –* Gallup 2013) conducted in 140 countries in 2011 and 2012, only 13 percent of the labor force is "engaged" while 63 percent is "not engaged" and 24 percent is "actively disengaged." At a moment in which businesses should be making the most of the creativity and intelligence of their workers to better compete in an ever-faster and increasingly complex and globalized world, a hefty 87 percent of the labor force is not engaged in business activity. Our various investigations of the situations we find with our clients organizations sadly support the Gallup findings.

Today we live in a state of volatility, uncertainty, complexity and ambiguity, a "VUCA" world:

- **Volatility**: Tending towards accentuated and unpredictable variations;
- **Uncertainty**: A lack of precision and clarity. Insufficient knowledge;
- **Complexity**: A qualitative trait of a system causing it to take on characteristics not derived from the straightforward juxtaposition of its components;
- **Ambiguity**: Open to wide interpretation.

Working in a "VUCA world" requires an entire range of new skills, including the ability to improve and constantly reinvent one's own way of thinking, operating and solving problems new and old, with creativity and imagination, thereby increasing the range of possibilities at our disposal.

The future is not a simple, linear extension of the past. Instead, the future is increasingly taking new and unforeseen trajectories. A leader must develop competencies suited to working in environments characterized by ever more rapid transformation and unclear boundaries.

Effective, efficient and fast teamwork, for instance, will become a distinctive marker of successful organizations. Continuous learning, for executives as well as workers, will be something to cultivate with concentration and discipline.

Technological development and business dynamics (market, competitors) are represented by an exponential curve shown in

Figure 1. The world is becoming faster, more complex, interconnected and globalized. These tendencies will only continue to accelerate over time. An interesting example of this is the development of the computational power of computers.

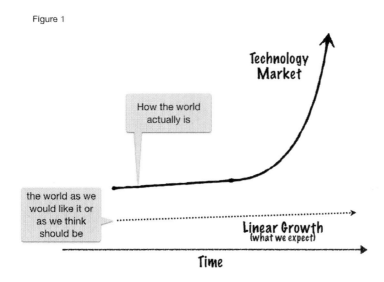

Figure 1

This passage from "Why Design Matters More than Moore" (John Maeda, *The Wall Street* Journal, 22 May 2015), summarizes the acceleration of technology over time:

> "**The transformative power of Moore's Law**. Until the last few years, the solution to every new problem in tech has been simple: more technology. There's a good reason for this. Computers, when first developed, had a fraction of the power they have today. For example, 15 years ago we were astonished to hear that the Furby toy had more computing power than the machines that launched the Apollo missions to space.
>
> To put Moore's Law, which recently celebrated its 50th anniversary, in context, 1*2 is 2, 2*2 is 4, 4*2 is 8, and 8*2 is 16. So in six years – which consists of four periods of Moore's Law – you get a 16x increase. Make that 12 years and it's a 256x increase. Make it 24 years and you get

a 65,536x increase. And in 36 years? The increase is 8,388,608x. So next year, in 2016, you can expect the computer you'll be using to be 8.3 million times more powerful than the one you were using in 1980. It's just mind-boggling.

Nanotechnologies, genetic engineering, virtual reality, wearable tech, the Internet of Things (network of physical objects or "things" embedded with electronics, software, sensors, and connectivity to enable objects to exchange data with the manufacturer, operator and/or other connected devices – Wikipedia), and many other new technological "contraptions" will profoundly modify our world and produce a whole array of new needs, social behaviors and business models.

How will this affect the way companies are going to need to be managed? Current management theories and processes are shown in Figure 2 as a flat line:

Figure 2

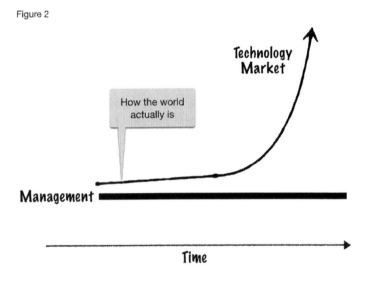

It has been years now since there was any real innovation in management theory, and so the distance between flat management models, which is to say "obsoletes" (the cause) and technological, social and economic development, creates a gap which explains the many difficulties (the effects) many companies find themselves facing (Figure 3).

Figure 3

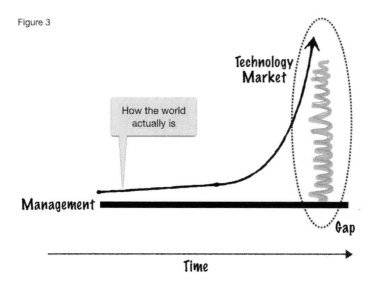

In fact, many businesses are using old-fashioned management tools and instruments no different essentially to those in use some thirty or forty years ago. Speed back then was unlike speed today, moving the time and at the same pace as the Internet.

A study conducted by the Institute for the Future, "Future Work Skills 2020," offers a range of interesting perspectives regarding the key skills we will need over the coming years:

> "Global connectivity, smart machines and new media are just some of the drivers reshaping how we think about work, what constitutes work and the skills we will need to be productive contributors in the future."

The study identifies six drivers – big disruptive shifts that are likely to reshape the future landscape – that are going to result in radical change:

- **Extreme Longevity**: Increasing global lifespans change the nature of careers and learning;
- **Rise of Smart Machines and Systems**: Workplace automation nudges human workers out of rote, repetitive tasks;
- **Computational World**: Massive increases in sensors and processing power make the world a programmable system;
- **New Media Ecology**: New communication tools require new media literacies beyond text;
- **Superstructured Organizations:** Social technologies drive new forms of production and value creation;
- **Globally Connected World**: Increased global interconnectivity puts diversity and adaptability at the center of organizational operations.

Changes will be a consequence of a confluence of various drivers which, combining their effects, will produce "true disruptions." The study goes on to define a range of new competencies that the leaders of tomorrow will have to acquire in order to manage these radical changes:

- **Sense-Making**: Ability to determine the deeper meaning or significance of what is being expressed;
- **Social Intelligence**: Ability to connect to others in a deep and direct way, to sense and stimulate reactions and desired interactions;
- **Novel and Adaptive Thinking**: Proficiency at thinking and coming up with solutions and responses beyond that which is rote or rule-based;
- **Cross-Cultural Competency**: Ability to operate in different cultural settings;
- **Computational Thinking**: Ability to translate vast amounts of data into abstract concepts and to understand data-based reasoning;
- **New Media Literacy**: Ability to critically assess and develop content that uses new media forms , and to leverage these media for persuasive communication;

- **Transdisciplinarity**: Literacy in and ability to understand concepts across multiple disciplines;
- **Design Mindset**: Ability to represent and develop tasks and work processes for desired outcomes;
- **Cognitive Load Management**: Ability to discriminate and filter information for importance, and to understand how to maximize cognitive functioning using a variety of tools and techniques;
- **Virtual Collaboration**: Ability to work productively, drive engagement, and demonstrate presence as a member of a virtual team.

A quick glance at this list of new skills should suffice to see how most training is, in fact, already obsolete way before it is carried out; looking backwards to the past instead of into the future. It is like teaching Morse code to people who use the latest generation computers every day to navigate the Internet.

Many business running training programs right now remain stuck in Excel or PowerPoint courses or on dated leadership courses. And, in many companies there is no training because it is seen as a cost, as diverting energies from daily tasks deemed more important than knowledge acquisition, which, conversely, could instead be the deciding factor in sealing a company's future.

Management today is suffering from a range of chronic difficulties; a lack of vision, problems with people management and in engaging the best in people, an inability to work in dynamic markets. Management today has constructed working environments that do not stimulate creativity or encourage initiative-taking, which employs anachronistic management models, is in many instances devoid of creativity and imagination, seeks short term results, proposes values in which nobody really believes and objectives that are neither stimulating or meaningful.

Current management models are no longer suitable for successfully facing the challenges of the twenty first century. The profound changes described above in technology, markets and social customs require us to radically rethink how managers work and act and to reconsider the processes and instruments they will need to be equipped with so as to create a culture that is genuinely new in the companies they steer. This means that less management and more leadership will be required.

Bob and I agree on the need for the development of different models and behaviors as well as on the value of individuals in companies as a real strategic asset. It is in fact on new abilities that We are working together to produce a whole series of new ideas and initiatives that will comprise the mindset of tomorrow's leaders.

Bob is an original thinker who has made a huge contribution to the development of a range of new ideas on management and leadership processes. Many have drawn from his work without affording him recognition for having had the courage to describe, study, and investigate what lay beyond the obvious, as accepted by the majority, and design a range of innovative contributions on the themes of business and organizational leadership.

Bob's idea of leadership as a process deserves to be studied, contemplated, and, above all, applied so that we can create open environments in which individuals can make a contribution. Environments where continuous learning is an operational rule, applied constantly in order to enable entire organizations to evolve in which leaders can really make a difference by improving themselves and their teams every day, steadfastly and unceasingly.

In an ever-faster world, Speed Leadership really is "a better way to lead."

Enjoy reading,

Massimo Torinesi
Business Designer
Heiko Xplore – Italy
www.heikoxplore.com

Preface

I am happy to bring to you what I believe is a true breakthrough in how to better comprehend leadership and how to improve leadership skills and capabilities: Speed Leadership. This practical new approach takes a *process* view of leadership in preference to long-standing view of leadership based on personality, behaviors, authenticity, and so on.

Understanding leadership from a process perspective differs substantially from how leadership is normally viewed or taught. The traditional human resources approach to leadership is rooted in organizational behavior, organizational development, and leadership development derived from academic theories that focus on unique personal characteristics or the life stories of executives. This renders leadership as subjective and more in the realm of art than science. While they are not wrong, these traditional ways of understanding and improving leadership have been largely ineffective. Viewing leadership as processes creates a new, practical, and more scientific basis for understanding and improving leadership.

In general, there continues to be substantial dissatisfaction with leadership among the workers in organizations due to factors such as the near-automatic response to blame people when things go wrong; devotion to time-killing, distracting, and wasteful organizational politics; chronically poor leadership; and the continued acceptance of sub-criminal psychopaths in leadership positions.

In general, the leadership needs of employees are not being met. Without question, it is reasonable for followers to expect far better leadership skills and capabilities than they have experienced. Poor leadership has consequences with respect to short-term needs, the long-term survival of the organization, prosperity among stakeholders, employee turnover, and the physical and mental health of workers.

For all the benefits that great leadership offers, the process of becoming a great leader remains too difficult. Sincere efforts are often undercut by norms of organizational behavior that reduce leadership to micromanaging people, attention to irrelevant details, short-term focus, unreachable goal-setting, kicking ass, and reliance on heroic acts to fix everyday problems.

Speed Leadership is the result of more than 15 years of research and teaching new, progressive ways of comprehending and practicing leadership. The iterative process of research and teaching, as well as my own years of experience in industry as a leader, has yielded innumerable useful insights into the differences between traditional and progressive leadership. This book presents practical solutions to long-standing problems experienced by organizations steeped in traditional leadership.

The focus is on leadership within an organization, though it includes leadership as it pertains to stakeholders external to the organization such as suppliers, customers, investors, and communities. The leadership processes examined are common, day-to-day processes that all leaders engage in, and which profoundly affect followers and their ability to do their work.

This book seeks to inform, educate, and motivate current and future leaders to improve their leadership skills and capabilities by understanding and improving their leadership processes. In the process view of leadership, processes get the blame for problems, not people. However, it is incumbent upon leaders to recognize and act upon all improvement opportunities, just as they advise, if not require, workers to do. Leaders must be willing to confront process-oriented criticism whose objective is to help them improve and become more effective leaders. Criticism without identifying pathways for improvement is not helpful. This book identifies simple pathways for improvement that are specific, actionable, and effective.

Speed Leadership will help leaders think differently about their role as leaders and begin the transition to leading with greater precision and effectiveness. Similar to way in which people learn to play a musical instrument, the production of customer-pleasing sounds are the result of daily practice – thinking and doing. It is the same with Speed Leadership; you must commit to daily practice to produce employee-pleasing leadership.

This book strives to make clear the connection between improved leadership processes and improving the health of all employees. Poor leadership causes chronic stress, which results in physical and mental health problems among employees. Good leadership has the opposite effect; happy employees who enjoy their work, are more engaged, and contribute steady streams of ideas and innovations that all organizations desperately need in order to satisfy customers and prosper.

Readers should recognize Speed Leadership as an important new element to existing employee wellness programs. In addition to wellness programs such as smoking cessation, exercise, weight loss, nutrition and diet, etc., add to that leadership process improvement. Instead of a stress management program for employees, imagine stress reduction and stress elimination throughout the organization due to good leadership resulting from improved leadership processes. Imagine, also, not just the healthcare cost savings, but the many opportunities that will present themselves as a result of great leadership.

I believe that leaders with an open mind, a willing heart, and genuine concern for the long-term success of the business and its stakeholders, will find this book to be extremely helpful, at minimum, if not life-changing.

Putting into practice the concepts and methods presented in *Speed Leadership* will lead to better human and business outcomes, as well as great pride and satisfaction in your work as a leader.

Bob Emiliani
July 2015
Wethersfield, Conn.

Introduction

This book has at its foundation the practical concept of, and business need for, information flow. It is a central feature of Speed Leadership because of its great importance in determining the true health of an organization at any point in time. What leaders must avoid is organizational atherosclerosis – restricted or blocked information flow – because it is deadly. Instead of accumulating fatty material (cholesterol) on artery walls, organizations accumulate defensive routines in their business and decision-making processes. This is unhealthy, and will, without doubt, result in serious and expensive problems related to important product lines or the business itself.

Understanding Speed Leadership begins by adopting the view that organizations are information processing hubs regulated by leaders and a system of management. The two regulate various resources such as time, money, material, information, equipment, people, physical space, etc. These resources can be used in ways that are efficient, inefficient, or somewhere in between, depending upon the management system used.

Traditional management is rooted in inefficient batch-and-queue information processing, in which batches of information are processed and then sit in queues for long periods of time.

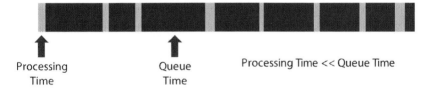

Processing Time   Queue Time   Processing Time << Queue Time

All organizations that use batch-and-queue information processing have significant information flow problems. It is important to understand what "information" means. Information is commonly understood to be conversations, spreadsheets, software, data, charts, forms, presentations, signs and symbols, etc. In Speed Leadership, physical objects such as material (e.g. raw material, work-in-process, finished goods, etc.) are considered to be information as well because they are defined by the information contained in blueprints and specifications.

Information flow improves when batch size is reduced and queues are reduced and eliminated. The result is higher fidelity information that is available more quickly, which, in turn results in decision-making that is both better quality and faster.

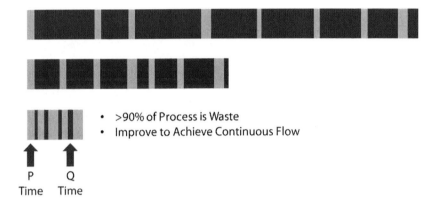

- >90% of Process is Waste
- Improve to Achieve Continuous Flow

P   Q
Time   Time

Various practical methods can be used to improve information flow in any physical or human business process. Notice in the image above that 90 percent or more of batch-and-queue processing is waste. This is true for any process, including leadership processes.

An organization's competitive advantage rests to a great degree on the timeliness and effectiveness of human information processing. Importantly, human information processing improves only when people (employees, suppliers, customers, investors, and communities) experience a positive outcome. The timeliness and effectiveness of human information processing are greatly reduced when people are harmed. Therefore, efforts to improve human information processing must be non-zero-sum (win-win) to have the greatest positive impact.

For example, people – whether employees, suppliers, customers, etc. – do not like to wait, and waiting causes additional problems for an organization. Improving information processing to reduce waiting by employees, yet which somehow results in more waiting for customers would not constitute an improvement. The outcome has to be reduced waiting for both employees and customers. Eliminating waiting in all processes will have the net result of improving customer satisfaction, and, in most cases, significantly improve the value proposition as well. This, in turn, can result in greater pricing power and higher market share.

Whether or not information flows depends not just on the technical aspects of how work is organized, but also the behavioral aspects of how people interact with one another. Therefore, process improvement directed towards improving information flow can only occur if people are respected. This is a fundamental requirement if leaders expect information to flow. "Shooting the messenger" is an example of not respecting people, which in turn severely distorts or shuts down the flow of information.

Employees (and suppliers) are not powerless. They use passive-aggressive (quietly obstructionist) behaviors to even the score with their leaders, which is bad for the organization and will eventually have a negative impact on employees as well. Passive-aggressive behaviors block information flow and result in delays and re-work. That zero-sum (win-lose) behavior is, of course, bad for both internal and external customers.

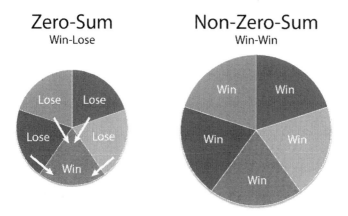

Human participants in information processing – employees, suppliers, customers, investors, or communities – desire non-zero sum (win-win) outcomes as a prerequisite for engagement and sharing of information. Nobody wants to be the loser, so why purposefully make someone the loser? The result will be impaired information flows that affect the ability of an organization to compete and make good decisions quickly.

People who are respected willingly do their part help in the processes to help make information flow. Organizations that have a "no-blame" policy for problems enjoy far better information flow than those who "shoot the messenger." People who experience the latter, either in obvious or subtle ways, will withhold information. They withhold information for many reasons, such as:

- Fear of being blamed for problems.
- Unaware or unsure of what information to share and when.
- Fear of appearing to not be in control or lacking competence.
- A belief that information is not to be shared (knowledge is power).
- Being publicly humiliated by their boss.

Traditional management practice, rooted in batch-and-queue information processing, does not have a strong process focus. Instead, the focus is on results, typically short-term, as captured by the phrases spoken by top leaders such as:

- "I don't care how you do it, just get it done."
- "Do whatever it takes."
- "Make it happen."
- "Failure is not an option."
- "Flawless execution."

Results, therefore, are often bad, and, in traditional management practice, people are blamed for bad results and other problems. When people are blamed for problems, it expands and institutionalizes batch-and-queue information processing within the organization and outward to suppliers and customers.

Information, therefore, flows less and less over time, and leaders spend their days firefighting instead of doing the work that they should be doing.

Leaders who think and act in ways that cause people to withhold information do a disservice to themselves and employees, as well as to suppliers, customers, and investors. Instead, leaders must develop a balanced focus on both process and results. The view that good processes yield good results is both simple and pragmatic.

It is critically important to comprehend work, including leaders' work, as processes and to understand the details of processes so that they can be improved. When results do not occur as expected, the process must be blamed, not the people. Today, it is common for employees to use structured problem-solving processes to understand the root cause of process problems and identify practical countermeasures to prevent their recurrence. Leaders must do the same.

Leaders typically do not recognize their day-to-day work as comprised of many different processes. Instead, they see their work as a series of disconnected activities performed as-needed to solve the day's biggest problems. The daily firefights further prevent leaders from having a process focus. Unfortunately, it is batch-and-queue information processing that is largely responsible for leaders' daily firefights.

Let's instead begin to understand leadership from a process perspective. What do leaders do? What processes do they participate in? Which processes do they have in common with other leaders? What are the core leadership processes? How many are there? In answering these questions, we find there are 15 core leadership processes that leaders are engaged in on a more-or-less daily basis. You will learn about these in Chapter 2.

What is the benefit of understanding leadership from a process perspective? It allows one to understand and correct problems in ways that could not be done previously. It allows one to identify specific errors made by leaders in relation to the processes the leaders are engaged in. How does one determine the errors that leaders make in their work processes? Simple; we find out by asking employees a question:

"What errors do leaders make in this leadership processes?"

Asking that question to employees for all 15 leadership processes yields an enormous amount of useful information. They have no trouble identifying dozens of leadership process errors for each of the 15 leadership processes. The key take-away is that leadership is an error-prone activity, not an error-free activity as perceived by most leaders.

Knowing the specific errors enables leaders to identify root causes where necessary and correct errors using the same structured problem-solving and process improvement routines that have become ubiquitous in most organizations today. Leadership processes can be improved and standardized in the same way that processes on the shop and office floors can be improved and standardized. This will result in better leadership: fewer errors, higher fidelity information, better decision-making, and more rapid response to changing conditions.

Leaders expect employees to be problem-solvers, and hopefully problem avoiders as well. Likewise, employees have the same expectations of their leaders. But, leaders cannot do that if they are unaware of the errors they make in their leadership processes.

The pages that follow examine the 15 leadership processes, errors associated with each leadership process, and practical pathways for improvement. I am confident that if you accept this information, think deeply about it, and make necessary improvements, you will experience positive outcomes that cannot be achieved any other way.

Questions For The Executive Team

Some important questions emerge from the Introduction:

- Why does nearly leader view the batch-and-queue method as an effective means of processing information?
- How has your organization's competitive advantage been harmed by poor information processing (i.e. late, incomplete, or missing information)?
- In what ways does your focus on results impair human information processing?
- What leadership behaviors inadvertently support batch-and-queue information processing and the reduction of human information processing capabilities?
- What has each member of the senior leadership done to eliminate organizational atherosclerosis – restricted or blocked information flow? What was the result?
- What has each member of the senior leadership done to improve information flow? What was the result?

Discuss these questions as a senior management team. Use structured problem-solving processes to answer these questions and provide direction for improvement. Summarize the results of the discussion and problem-solving in two or three flip-chart pages, and post them on a wall for further thought and analysis.

Thoughts, Observations, and Actions To Take

Thoughts, Observations, and Actions To Take

1

What Is Speed Leadership?

We live in a time of great social and technological change. The evidence surrounds us and engulfs us. Yet, one thing has remained nearly constant over the last 100 years: The manner in which most organizations and led and managed on a day-to-day basis. In most cases, the leadership is adequate, but not exceptional, as one would expect from educated and highly paid professionals. Often, the leadership is poor, yet the company prospers – at least for a while – because competitors are few or their leadership is even worse.

Employees have tired of leaders who push their ancient and ineffective leadership style onto them. They are tired of bad leadership and want better work experiences, free of politics, bureaucracy, blame, and organizational routines that slow things down and which give rise to chronic stress. They want leaders to be responsive to their pull, the pull of customers, and the pull of changing times. They want leaders to take improvement seriously and show real progress in how they lead. Expectations for leaders have changed.

Rapid technological change requires leadership thinking and practice that is commensurate with the times. Executives who lead as if it is 1915 serve all stakeholders poorly. Times have changed, and so must leadership. The speed of leadership must closely match the speed of change in technology and the market place, as well as expectations. The only way to do that is to eliminate both technical and behavioral errors in leadership processes.

What is Speed Leadership? It is not leaders who lead quickly, although that might be true. Rather, Speed Leadership is a method of leading that helps other people in the organization go fast. "Fast" means doing good work quickly and effectively, which is what most people strive to do but often cannot. "Fast" does not mean poor work done quickly, speeding people up, or other negative connotation. Speed Leadership does not burden people. It helps people. Whatever one's work happens to be, Speed Leadership makes the work go faster and better by eliminating the leadership technical and behavioral errors that cause confusion and re-work, increase batch sizes, and extend queue times. The result of Speed Leadership is better and more satisfying work that is completed in less time in response to the rapidly changing times that we live in.

Speed Leadership is a new design for leadership synchronized to the times we live in, if not to stay ahead of the times. It is an innovative leadership method for rapidly changing times, and which demands greater individual and organizational capacity for adapting to changing circumstances.

Naturally, Speed Leadership begins at the top. A CEO or president who thinks, behaves, and does their work in ways consistent with Speed Leadership is a role model for lower-level leaders to follow. This is by far the lowest cost and fastest way to train a leadership team and everyone else in the organization. Rapidly training followers in Speed Leadership is, itself, an aspect of Speed Leadership.

Speed Leadership cannot be mandated. It requires its practitioners to think and improve leadership processes continuously, resulting in outcomes that do good and never do harm. Speed Leadership must be the leaders' daily leadership practice.

In this new design for leadership, the key unit of measure for executives is time, not money. Speed Leaders are acutely aware of any belief, behavior, competency, or leadership process error that slows down the good work that employees do and want to do better. Leading on the basis of time creates new opportunities that are completely unavailable to those whose ancient mindset and methods require them to lead on the basis of money. The outcome, of course, will be much better financial and non-financial performance, due in part to better information, faster and better analysis and decision-making, and more rapid leadership process improvement cycles.

Fundamentally, Speed Leadership says the number one job of leadership is to get information to flow. That is the starting point for all that follows in terms of daily activities, behaviors, decision-making, strategy, execution, and so on. But, what is information flow?

Information flow in an organization is the time derivative of the supply of information. In mathematical terms, it is:

$$\text{Information Flow} = \frac{di}{dt}$$

The supply of information is low when organizational politics is great, which means that the flow of information over time will also be low. That is a bad situation, one that threatens the business and all other stakeholders. Organizational politics slows down, distorts, blocks, and otherwise destroys information flows, which, in turn, increases the number of problems and their severity. Employees hate organizational politics, and no customer benefits from it because it does not create value for them. It absorbs value by adding cost and consuming time.

If, instead, the supply of information is high due to the absence of organizational politics, then the flow of information over time will be great. That is good, and it sets the organization up for long-term success. Organizational politics must therefore be contained to levels low enough so as not to distort or disrupt information flows.

Mathematically, leadership can be expressed as:

$$\text{Leadership} = \frac{di}{dt}$$

where information, i, is continuously increasing over time, t.

Thus, in Speed Leadership, the core function of leadership is time and information to flow, for the purpose of quickly recognizing and effectively responding to problems.

The figures on the next page illustrate the difference between information and information flow for conventional leaders who accept the existence of organizational politics (Slow Leadership, Figure 1) and leaders who improve leadership processes to reduce organizational politics and gain the trust of employees (Speed Leadership, Figure 2).

The information supply in Figure 1 increases slowly and linearly over time, while information flow (di/dt) remains steady over time. As a result, information flow is static; there is no improvement over time. Consequently, leaders face a never-ending repetition of problems and nasty unwanted surprises.

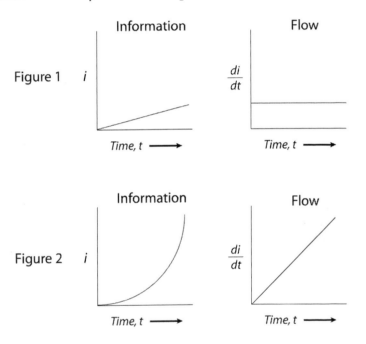

The information supply in Figure 2 increases rapidly over time, as does information flow, which increases over time. As a result, information flow is growing; there is improvement over time. Consequently, leaders experience fewer surprises and whose negative impact is smaller. In summary:

$$\text{Leadership} = \frac{di}{dt}$$

In other words,

Leadership = Information Flow

Better leadership results in better information flow. However, personality, behaviors, or authenticity alone will do it, nor will HR improvement tools such as leadership competency models. Leaders must instead identify the specific technical and behavioral errors in leadership processes that result in batching of information and expansion of queue time, and how to eliminate them.

Substantially improving the fidelity of information is of paramount importance for a business to avoid costly problems and to survive. Equally important is the time-frame in which information is bounded. An organization heavy with organizational politics changes the nature of time from hours, minutes, and seconds, months, weeks, and days, as shown in the image below. "Company Time" is Slow Leadership.

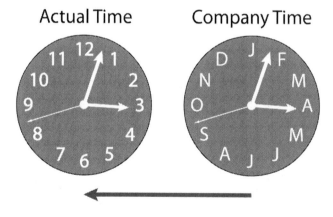

This image illustrates why organizations are often late to understand and respond to changes in employees, supplier, or customer wants and needs. Organizational politics slows down the clock and yields a company time that is far slower than the actual time. The goal is to move "Company Time" to the left towards "Actual Time." Actual Time is Speed Leadership.

In addition to reducing organizational politics, eliminating leadership process errors improves leadership credibility, trust, and effectiveness, as well as teamwork and employee engagement. It transforms leadership into a skilled professional activity.

Finally, think of this: What is the type of leader that employees revere, that suppliers respect, that customers appreciate, that investors cheer, and which makes communities proud? It is leaders who have advanced from turning people into losers to making everyone a winner. From a practical perspective, win-win outcomes are almost never perfect (though sometimes they are), yet leaders strive to achieve balance that ensures information flow. A useful way to think about it is as follows: Nobody wins as much as they would like, but nobody loses as much as they could. The mindset and practices that yield win-win outcomes are fundamental features of Speed Leadership.

In the next chapter you will learn how leaders' work can be broken down into fifteen core processes that have information as their raw material, and how errors in leadership processes distort and block information flow. In Chapter 3, you will learn how leadership errors and blocked information flow cause employee suffering, which, in turn, leads to employee health problems and poor job performance. Following that, you will create standards for each of the 15 leadership processes and learn how to improve leadership processes.

Questions For The Executive Team

Some important questions emerge from Chapter 1:

- What are the consequences of leadership that causes distraction, confusion, and created unneeded stress for employees?
- How does changing our view of leadership from personality, behaviors, and authenticity to time and information affect each one of these stakeholders: employees, suppliers, customer, investors, and the communities in which we operate?
- How do leaders' personality and behaviors affect their ability to sense and respond to problems and opportunities? How are these improved if leaders instead focus on time and information flow?
- How do time and information flow affect our ability to achieve strategic objectives?
- After a period of time spent on leadership process improvement, should the company part ways with the worst, most error-prone leaders (and psychopaths) at all levels, despite their appearance of effectiveness?

Discuss these questions as a senior management team. Use structured problem-solving processes to answer these questions and provide direction for improvement. Summarize the results of the discussion and problem-solving in two or three flip-chart pages, and post them on a wall for further thought and analysis.

Thoughts, Observations, and Actions To Take

Thoughts, Observations, and Actions To Take

2

Leadership Processes

What is that leaders do every day? Fundamentally, they are information nodes. They receive, process, and convey information. And, they do this in every process that they are a part of. What are those processes? There are 15 leadership processes that make up the bulk of what leaders do on a daily basis. The leadership processes are:

1. Leading and managing people
2. Planning and budgeting
3. Workload management
4. Decision-making
5. Problem recognition and response
6. Problem solving
7. Management reviews (finance, operations, HR, etc.)
8. Employee feedback and coaching
9. Team meetings
10. Asking questions, listening, and receiving feedback
11. Information sharing
12. Developing people
13. Performance appraisal
14. Walking around, "go see"
15. Stakeholder engagement (customers, suppliers, investors, communities)

Things can go right and things can go wrong in any process. If many more things go right than wrong in each of these leadership processes, then we could characterize leadership as highly capable and effective. Unfortunately, many more things go wrong with each one of these leadership processes than right, in large part because the processes are batch-and-queue. Multiplied by the number of leaders in an organization, the total number of errors occurring every day is enormous and the unfavorable impacts on employees are widespread. It is not surprising, therefore, that employees in most organizations are not satisfied with their leadership.

You may be satisfied with your leadership, but you should not be. Professionalism demands that you be more critical of your performance as a leader in the same way that professional musicians are self-critical.

The problem is not that leaders make mistakes, because, after all, that is how people learn. The problem is to not recognize and correct errors. The greater problem is exposing followers (and other stakeholders) to the same errors over and over again, year after year. The massive problem that results from the errors is distorted and blocked information flow. This is harmful to the heath of the organization and the people in it.

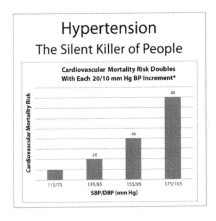

Think about this: What is the hallmark of professionalism? Consider professional athletes, musicians, dancers, or pharmacists, for example. The hallmark of professionalism is the absence of errors. Professionals make few errors, while amateurs make many errors. As a professional leader, the expectation is that you should make very few errors. Specifically, the number and severity of errors decrease over time as leaders' proficiency increases through daily practice, resulting in the delivery of a consistently high-quality leadership service to employees. As a leader, you will have to contend with both actual errors and perceived errors. Remember, leadership process errors are the result of process problems, not people problems.

Let's examine the errors that can be made in each one of the 15 leadership processes:

1. Leading and Managing People

There are at least 32 errors that can be made in this leadership process:

Failing to define people's role, failing to make expectations clear, insulting people (in front of others), picking favorite employees, using inappropriate language, micromanaging, blaming people for mistakes, ignoring one's role in causing the mistake, reacting first / thinking second, telling coworkers about your personal life, not being available to discuss process problems, being dismissive, yelling at employees, not being approachable, not encouraging teamwork, failing to command subordinates' respect, pick the same person to lead teams, insufficient definition of job responsibilities, not utilizing people's skills, giving unclear or mixed messages, not setting goals, communicating poorly, making disrespectful comments, ignoring procedures, not seeing the big picture, allowing poor performers to ignore policies without repercussion, staying in one's office, not spending time with new employees, lacking enthusiasm, low pay, bullying subordinates.

2. Planning and Budgeting

There are at least 30 errors that can be made in this leadership process:

Lengthy processes, faulty estimates, misallocation of resources, non-allocation of resources, making bad or uneducated decisions, no planning, not accepting inputs from subordinates, missed deadlines, errors in documents, spending budget for the sake of spending the budget, buying more than required, making items to forecast, not budgeting for needed items, cutting staff, not having a back-up plan, budget errors, under-budgeting, over-budgeting, setting unrealistic goals, poor allocation of human resources, running out of budget, poor planning, questioning every detail, insufficient time given to budgeting, ignore marketplace information, set people up to fail, indiscriminate cutting, unrealistic schedule, ignoring problems, extensive re-work, keeping zombie projects alive.

3. Workload Management

There are at least 20 errors that can be made in this leadership process:

Taking on more projects than can be handled at one time, assigning more work than a worker can handle, showing no appreciation for handling heavy workloads, assuming that extra workload will be accepted, creating bottlenecks when only one person can do a particular type of work, not allocating labor resources where they are needed most, asking people to produce more product than is humanly possible, constant firefighting due to poor planning, no time for manager to meet with staff, not telling their boss that a goal or objective cannot be met, unevenly distributing workload, giving too little work, giving work to someone without the skills to do it, giving the same job to two people, assigning workload to a favorite worker, supervisors trying to do all the work themselves, unconstrained workload growth (never say "no"), overloading workers during vacation or holiday periods, misjudging the time for executing projects, lacking manpower due to cost-cutting.

4. Decision-Making

There are at least 24 errors that can be made in this leadership process:

Directing employees to other people for approvals (to avoid responsibility), over-committing and under-delivering, making promises that cannot be kept, late decisions, making people wait, not listening to employee input, making decisions solely on financial concerns, making bad decisions, irresponsible decisions made by ignoring certain information, jumping to conclusions about the cause of a problem, making decisions based on erroneous data or metrics, decisions made quickly without adequate deliberation, decisions driven by short-term thinking, rushed decisions, blaming subordinates for bad decisions, not exploring alternative paths, stopping at the first usable idea, not seeking additional information, making uninformed decisions, postponing decisions based on an excuse (e.g. lack of information), decisions that result in arguments among team members, listening to inputs from experienced employees and ignoring inputs from lower-level employees, overconfidence in one's decisions, irrational decisions.

5. Problem Recognition and Response

There are at least 17 errors that can be made in this leadership process:

Unwillingness to learn about or confront problems, lack of involvement in problems, late response to problems, not wanting to change ("we have always done it this way"), overreact to problems, faulty response to problems, failure to question the data or ask "is this all the data?", jumping to conclusions, blaming people instead of blaming the process, not asking employees their opinions about a problem, not recognizing that a problem exists even when told about it, not acting on the problem, problem lingers uncorrected until it becomes too big to ignore, not identifying risks (future problems) before they happen, downplaying the size or scope of an issue, holding lengthy unproductive meetings about a problem, seeking to blame someone for the problem.

6. Problem Solving

There are at least 20 errors that can be made in this leadership process:

Waiting for new technology or automation (expensive fixes), performing a faulty root-cause analysis, seeking the one best answer on the first try, not asking for input on problems, micromanage problem-solving, failure to see the much larger process problem, overreact to solve problems quickly vs. correctly, problem recurs due to short-term thinking and quick-fix mentality, not using a team to solve process problems, blaming people instead of investigating and correcting a problem, laissez-faire approach to problem solving, resisting problem-solving methods used and solutions identified, not properly defining the problem, ignoring potential solutions, waiting for problem to solve itself, causing delays by debating various solutions, delegating problem-solving to lower-level employees, not following the problem-solving process, spending more time discussing problem than solving it, acting defensive about problems.

7. Management Reviews (finance, operations, HR, etc.)

There are at least 31 errors that can be made in this leadership process:

Time-consuming review preparation, complicated or confusing review processes, people unsure of expectations, micromanaging finance/accounting targets, faulty information, positive feedback for favorite people, conflict of interests, not having all the necessary data, biased views, skewing statistics to make them look better then they are, not giving clear or honest feedback, not focusing on how to improve in areas, leader gives team member biased information, reviews based on metrics that have been gamed to show progress or improvement, no reviews, focusing on people (not process), pitting one department against another, reviews fail to reveal or address problems, unfocused, superficial, softball questions, blame or admonish for misses, praise for being lucky, focusing on one negative event and ignore good work, hostile tone, reading e-mail during reviews (rudeness), lengthy discussions on irrelevant items, politicking to look better than is actually the case, frequent re-scheduling, use as a way to discipline employees.

8. Employee Feedback and Coaching

There are at least 21 errors that can be made in this leadership process:

One-way feedback (manager to worker), no feedback, management never opens the suggestion box, feedback not timely, lack of training on how to give specific and constructive feedback, little or no training on how to coach people, use anger as means to give feedback, insufficient feedback, not allowing people to explain the problem at hand, feedback/coaching given only to staff whose work the manager understands, feedback not given with empathy, perfunctory feedback (does not really care about what you do), not giving honest feedback, not giving employees one-on-one time with managers, not discussing areas of improvement, focusing only on the negative, negative coaching, high variation in coaching (from great to non-existent), no standard way to give feedback, focus on faults vs. accomplishments, unconstructive criticism, blaming employees for errors.

9. Team Meetings

There are at least 32 errors that can be made in this leadership process:

Not showing up, constantly rescheduling meetings, manager arrives late (causing re-work), doesn't respond to employees' concern, becomes a bullshitting session, only done when the manager has time/something to say, doesn't allow for honest employee feedback, meetings go off-topic, simple problems not resolved, talks down to team members, team members intimidated by leader (too scared to bring up important topics), attendance limited to work that the manager understands, top down meeting, questions not asked, people scared to say something or share ideas, leader's ideas prevail, meetings are sporadic and poorly attended, dismissing people's ideas, wasting people's time, not having an agenda, not inviting crucial people, opportunity to speak is limited (leader monopolizes the conversation), certain individuals are out of the loop, allowing meeting to degrade into a shouting match, vague agendas, agendas established on short notice, always a problem (someone is missing, the leader is late, information not available), time-consuming discussions, no following-up, taking calls during team meetings, texting during team meetings, side conversations.

10. Asking Questions, Listening, and Receiving Feedback

There are at least 32 errors that can be made in this leadership process:

Not asking questions, asking confrontational or intimidating questions, responding before allowing someone to finish speaking, cutting off employee responses, not listening, ignoring feedback, showing anger when asking questions, fear of looking weak or indecisive, insincere request for feedback, not answering questions in a timely or effective manner, ask questions only when problems arise, punishing dissenters, having a closed door policy, cursing, insulting, manager's opinion prevails despite accurate feedback, turn everything into a negative, felt humiliated by asking questions, closed to change or new ideas, fluff or irrelevant questions; using poor word choices, judging people, not listening, not taking any action items, misinterpreting, cutting people off, blaming people, allowing distractions, de-valuing voice due to department or rank, insincere requests for feedback, ignoring feedback, ignoring suggestions, not following up.

11. Information Sharing

There are at least 25 errors that can be made in this leadership process:

Perfunctory, withhold information from employees (to maintain power, get credit for fixing problems, insecure, etc.), late to share information, give out unclear information, withhold information about problems or opportunities, shared if deemed necessary, not sharing information with other departments, sharing incorrect information or disinformation, sharing information only with favorite people, information sharing on subjective "need to know" basis (undercuts teamwork), hogging vital data, "not my job" mentality, unorganized information, information sharing seen as a disadvantage, compartmentalizing information, lack of information sharing during critical events, hoarding information to retain one's job, poor flow of information, using information that is inaccurate, incomplete, filtered, or outdated, withholding information to protect personal interests, bad information (that leads to incorrect activities or actions), confusing or conflicting information.

12. Developing People

There are at least 21 errors that can be made in this leadership process:

Denying training or development requests, does not develop people, passive approach, general vs. specific development, teaching people wrong things (pass on their own bad behaviors), does not like to develop people (fearing they will leave or want more money), believing career development is in hands of employees, does not allow cross training, development meetings take place infrequently (annually or twice per year), promoting favorites instead of people who work hard to develop themselves, not showing people how to do better (not setting positive example), would rather hire from outside than develop employees, developing wrong people for certain positions, being over-zealous about developing people (spend too much time and money), developing people in one's own (faulty) image, development opportunities available only for certain positions/levels, development only on personal time, few opportunities for development, developing wrong people, give training opportunities to favorites, delegating responsibility to training department or to employees (self-development).

13. Performance Appraisal

There are at least 17 errors that can be made in this leadership process:

Giving too much negative feedback at once, incorrect feedback (favorable or unfavorable) due to lack of awareness of performance, evaluating people based on forced quota system (top 10%), lack of training on how to do performance reviews properly, performed annually or semi-annually (vs. more frequent reviews/feedback), not sharing ways that employee could improve, getting defensive when employee questions rating, getting defensive when employees ask for more guidance, organizational politics dictate who gets a good review, not doing performance appraisals, biased appraisals, not accounting for total performance, appraisal unrelated to actual performance, not conforming to company performance appraisal policy, performance appraisal results same for all employees, lack of recognition for good performance, performance based narrowly on key business metrics.

14. Walking Around, "Go See"

There are at least 25 errors that can be made in this leadership process:

Only done when problems arise, stay in office, understanding of what is going on based on erroneous perceptions/information, focus walk-arounds on finding slackers vs. actually caring about employees and the work they do, always walk around with entourage (to explain/interpret), employees exhibit desired behavior only when being observed, not asking questions, look for people or things to blame, not visible due to workload mismanagement, stay ensconced in the executive area, prefer to "see" things through reports and presentations, use as means to micromanage, rarely in the building, not seen as a leadership activity, pretending to be interested in employees and their work, excessive focus on the numbers, seeing the wrong things, perfunctory visits to the workplace, fail to observe, fail to ask questions, does not understand the process, does not see problems, too little conversation, too much socializing, micromanaging.

15. Stakeholder Engagement (customer, supplier, investor, community)

There are at least 22 errors that can be made in this leadership process:

Failure to engage or solicit feedback from customers, employees and suppliers, negative perception of all suppliers, unresponsive to stakeholders, engage with all stakeholders except employees, low engagement, focus mainly on investors (unless must react to other group when a problem occurs), placing unrealistic expectations on suppliers, not handling customer complaints quickly and effectively, stakeholder responsiveness varies according to urgency, zero-sum outcomes for some stakeholders, not getting feedback, aloofness, negative attitudes towards certain stakeholders, stakeholder engagement not a priority, poor communication, rushed response to stakeholder demands, personal achievements trump stakeholders' interests, insincere concern for customers, lecture or criticize stakeholders, unethical treatment of stakeholders, blame stakeholders for problems, focus on only one stakeholder, lack of respect for stakeholders.

As you can see, a lot can go wrong in each one of the 15 leadership processes. These errors show that leaders have not mastered the basics. If you are honest, you will acknowledge making many, if not most of these errors at various times in your career. The point here is not to blame or judge, but instead to motivate leaders to improve.

The data cannot be ignored. The sheer number of errors should shock you into realizing that leadership is an error-prone activity in which a leader – one with professional aspirations – would be highly motivated to take action to improve. Imagine if you were a musician making these many mistakes. The sound would be unbearable. Or, a golfer. You would never finish 18 holes. Leaders must eliminate these errors to be considered professional.

At least 368 errors were identified for the 15 leadership processes. However, that does not include the hundred or more errors that leaders can make with respect to word choice, body language, facial expressions, tone of voice, inflection, nervous habits, inattentiveness due to multitasking, etc. Nor does it include errors in job interview, succession planning, or other leadership processes. There are perhaps 500 significant, fundamental errors that leaders can make in the 15 leadership processes, and possibly as many as 1000 unique errors in total. Leaders ask employees to ask a simple question: "How can I improve my process?" Leaders must ask that same simple question of themselves.

What are the effects of these leadership process errors on employees? Do these errors make them happy? Do employees ask leaders for more errors to make them even happier? Do these errors help focus employees' attention on their work and how to improve it? Do leadership errors make them more creative and innovative? Do they put employees at ease? No, they do not. The effect of many errors is to give employees the impression of amateur leadership, due to the resulting distractions, confusion, re-work, frustration, conflict, and job dissatisfaction.

None of the errors listed are difficult or complicated for leaders to make. These are basic leadership process errors that occur day after day, week after week, month after month, and year after year. Executives would go crazy if workers made as many basic errors in their work as they do.

What do these errors suggest is actually being managed in organizations? These errors suggest that numbers and results are being managed, not people and processes. It is no surprise that information flows are perpetually distorted or blocked, and widened or unclogged only when circumstances require it – usually, in emergencies.

The errors contribute to an organizational culture that blames people for problems. This, in turn, creates wasteful internal politics, re-work, and time delays as people seek to preserve and protect their personal or department interests. Time delays, in particular, are of great importance because most organizations serve competitive buyers' markets (or compete for resources in the case of not-for-profit organizations). Internal politics, re-work, and time delays are unaffordable luxuries.

In error-prone, batch-and-queue information processing organizations, people have difficulty seeing the actual situation, which translates into time delays. Immediately upon entering the company, the clock speed changes from hours, minutes, and seconds, and reads in months, weeks, and days. In dysfunctional organizations, decisions that should be made quickly drag on for months because people seek to avoid making decisions for fear of being blamed. Workers and managers are frustrated, confusion reigns, and people (employees, suppliers, customer, investors, and communities) are unhappy. Their interests, mostly shared, can never be satisfied using the traditional tools and methods to improve leadership.

Your competitors, however, are probably delighted at your dysfunctional information processing. They are delighted that you cannot compete as well as you could, and that it takes you too long and costs too much to develop new products and services. And, when you finally do release them to market, they miss the mark in fulfilling customer wants and needs.

Your organization is at a great disadvantage if it delights competitors more than it delights its customers. Meanwhile, the marketplace clock reads hours, minutes, and seconds. Think of it in a way that is similar to employee performance appraisals:

- **Company clock in hours, minutes, seconds:**
  Fully competent. Able to compete on marketplace time (flow). Continue efforts to improve.

- **Company clock in days, hours, minutes:**
  Development needed. Has difficulty competing on marketplace time. Corrective action required.

- **Company clock in months, weeks, and days:**
  Unsatisfactory performance. Unable to compete on marketplace time (batch-and-queue processing). Major corrective action required. May go out of business soon.

You cannot close the gap between your company's clock and the market's clock by squeezing: e.g. by overloading employees with work, by asking employees to work harder, by eliminating layers of management, by laying off employees, by outsourcing work, or by financial engineering. You have to look inward for the sources of your problems, in a non-blaming and non-judgmental way. Then you can make improvements every day.

Once again, recognize that leadership is an error-prone activity whose quality is therefore very poor. This contradicts the common view of leadership as intelligent, thoughtful, capable, and mostly free of errors. As a result, leaders have some hard work to do to improve the quality and effectiveness of the processes that they engage in. Senior managers who make few leadership process errors will create more lively and engaged teams. Those who make many leadership process errors will create a dysfunctional social environment whose work product is chronically poor.

Be assured that employees do not like to have their fate determined by leaders who make many fundamental errors in their core leadership processes. A fair question for employees to ask is: Are we suffering multiple bad consequences due to the many leadership process errors that our managers make?

From employees' perspective, leadership process errors are linked leadership behaviors, which act as a throttle. Value-added behaviors combined with few leadership process errors improve information flow. Wasteful behaviors combined with lots of leadership process errors decreases information flow. Think of all the additional problems caused by throttling between value-added behaviors and wasteful behaviors:

- Error-prone organization
- Difficulty seeing the actual situation
- Frustrated workers and managers
- Internal confusion (becomes contagious)
- Unhappy people (internal and external)

Leadership process errors are bad for organizations and bad for people.

It would be wise for leaders to consider leadership as a service (LaaS) to followers. Supervisors, middle-managers, and executives are suppliers of leadership services. The hundreds of leadership process errors shown previously provide clear evidence for the need to improve the leadership services.

In summary, the benefits of understanding leadership as processes is that it enables leaders to improve in ways that were not previously available to them. It is easier to identify specific errors, and the errors can be directly associated with process and results. Improvements can then be made using the different methods commonly found in organizations today.

In the next chapter, we will examine the different types of bad consequences that employees and the organization suffer as a result of leadership process errors.

Questions For The Executive Team

Some important questions emerge from Chapter 2:

- Why have we not thought of leadership as processes?
- Why did we miss this for so long?
- Who owns these leadership processes?
- What are the top 5 leadership processes where we make the most errors?
- Why do we lack professionalism?
- Why do we not see these mistakes?
- Why do we ignore facts?
- Why do we accept these problems?
- Why haven't we seen the need to improve?
- Why is it so hard for us to improve?
- In what ways has our formal education and corporate training failed us?
- What aspects of our formal education and corporate training have we failed to put into practice? Why?
- Do our leadership processes contain many defects in information processing due to biases, illogical thinking, and decision-making traps that affect all humans? What can we do to improve leadership information processing?
- Could the number of leadership process errors be used as a barometer to inform management, employees, and shareholders of the financial and non-financial health and wellness of the enterprise – and possibly a predictor of its future health as well?

Discuss these questions as a senior management team. Use structured problem-solving processes to answer these questions and provide direction for improvement. Summarize the results of the discussion and problem-solving in two or three flip-chart pages, and post them on a wall for further thought and analysis.

Thoughts, Observations, and Actions To Take

Thoughts, Observations, and Actions To Take

3

Consequences Of Leadership Process Errors

The hundreds of leadership process errors cited in Chapter 2 should be sufficient to motivate leaders at all levels to improve their leadership process, because, after all, they are role models for employees and responsible for all financial and non-financial processes and results. The errors help us understand the problem more thoroughly and point towards the direction of causes. We also need to clearly understand the human consequences of leadership process errors, with a particular focus on employees, as well as work-related consequences and how they affect the organization's ability to execute. This will provide additional motivation to improve.

Consider this: All leaders make leadership process errors, but who makes the most errors? It will be those leaders who are the least process focused. Who is the least process focused? It will be those leaders who are overcommitted or who just never thought much about processes. And, it will definitely be leaders who are political game-players, and, in the limit, corporate psychopaths. Most organizations tolerate the presence of politics and corporate psychopaths in leadership positions despite the many problems that they create because they are seen as people who are effective at getting things done. We will examine the impact that these leaders have on employees' mental and physical health, as well as the problems they create with respect to efforts to do good work quickly.

Importantly, a leader does not have to be highly political or a psychopath to create many problems for employees. The things that they say or do can have significant negative effects on employees. What organizations must seek to avoid is a chronic stress environment driven by psychopaths and psychopathic-like leaders, political game-players, unreachable goals, bad metrics, and by leadership process errors. I refer to these collectively as "bad leadership."

What is the effect of bad leadership on employee physical and mental health, and on how work gets done? The following lists were generated by actual employees of organizations. They were asked to cite bad effects that they personally experienced as a result of leadership process errors.

Mental Effects of Leadership Process Errors

- Depression
- Lost social connectivity
- Short-temper
- Intolerance for the leader
- Feeling belittled
- Stressful work environment
- Bring work issues home
- Question one's self and one's abilities
- Want to quit
- Nervous to confront leaders on issues
- Lack of work satisfaction
- Feeling that you can't do anything right
- Stress over job performance
- Anger over abusive treatment
- Feeling of helplessness
- Poor decision-making
- Humiliation
- Guilt
- Lower self-esteem
- Feeling unappreciated, incapable, and worthless
- Constantly worry about making a mistake
- Lack of confidence
- Confusion
- Humiliated in front of co-workers

- Low morale
- Discouraged
- Loss of motivation
- Feeling of inadequacy
- Reduced trust for others
- Anxiety and worry
- Office paranoia

None of these mental effects are what one would associate with doing good work, feeling valued, or being creative and innovative. They instead have the opposite effect. These bad mental effects are not indicative of responsible and professional leadership. Yet, it is common and leads to other unfavorable occurrences.

Employees who witness poor leadership that is rewarded with success will be left wondering if they need to be more superficial, political, or psychopath-like in order to get promoted. In other words, they will consider mirroring the leader's bad skills and behaviors in order to advance within the organization. No good can come from a perpetuation of negative mental effects driven by bad leadership.

Leaders speak of "speed to market," "low costs," and "teamwork." Bad leadership reduces speed to market, increases costs, and reduces teamwork. The traditional way of thinking about leadership does not provide the facts and means necessary to improve beyond mere words or a few new behaviors.

Physical Effects of Leadership Process Errors

- Stomach pain
- Acid reflux
- Weight gain
- Weight loss
- Always feeling tired
- Stress-related headaches
- Physical exhaustion

- Loss of sleep
- Nervousness, jitters
- Heart palpitations
- Muscle and neck pains
- Change in physical appearance
- Anxiety attacks
- Increased heart rate
- High blood pressure
- Feeling burned out
- Atherosclerosis
- Abdominal (visceral) fat
- Weakened immune system

These physical effects are the result of the existence of chronic stress caused by bad leadership. Acute stress is something we all have to deal with from time-to-time. Chronic stress, however, clearly has negative effects on human health, many of which accumulate slowly over time. Leaders' job descriptions do not require them to harm human health, so they should not do it.

Have a look at the list of medications prescribed to employees in the few years by therapeutic category such as cardiovascular, psychotherapeutic, gastrointestinal, cholesterol, etc. What are the top five prescribed medication categories in your company? What are the top five prescribed medication categories nationally? Are the two lists the same, or is your company's list different? Can you discern any correlation between prescription medication categories and the way the organization is led; meaning, poor leadership processes and leadership process errors that result in chronically stressful environments?

To be sure, many factors account for the prescription medications that employees require. But, is it possible that employee's medications reflect workplace conditions – at least to some measurable degree? It is possible, but unlikely, that there is zero correlation. Even if there is no probable correlation, the mental and physical effects that bad leadership can have on people must not be ignored because it impairs execution. If it is not costing the organization through higher healthcare expenses, sick days, etc., it is surely costing the organization in many other practical ways that affect its ability to innovate and respond rapidly to changes in the marketplace.

Work Effects of Leadership Process Errors

- Political decision-making
- Daily firefighting
- Lower work performance
- Reduced productivity
- Low morale
- Overloaded with work
- Poor concentration
- Lack of motivation
- Afraid to speak up
- Defective work
- Re-work
- Ideas and opinions are ignored
- Bullied into doing things
- Look for a job elsewhere
- Socially uncomfortable with co-workers
- Poor quality work
- Lack of trust
- Hostility towards others
- Avoid contact with others
- Less communication with co-workers
- Do work beyond job responsibilities
- Reduced teamwork

Absent any understanding of leadership processes and the hundreds of errors contained therein, one can easily understand leaders' frustration with workers and their ability to do good work in a timely manner. However, knowledge of leadership processes and the hundreds of errors contained therein means that leaders' frustrations with workers are totally misdirected.

The effect of bad leadership is to put the organization at great risk in many different ways, including the fundamental activity of employees doing the daily work that they are assigned to do. Leaders must not allow employees to struggle to do their daily work. They must simplify the complex and lead in ways that it easier for employees to do their daily work. There are other effects as well:

Other Effects of Leadership Process Errors

- Broken teamwork and trust
- Difficulty with home and family life
- Lack of purpose in workplace
- Changed personal relationships with friends
- Prone to make more mistakes
- Less effort put into work
- Unsatisfying work environment
- Second-guessing
- Feeling unable to solve work problems
- Poor decision-making
- Unresolved conflicts
- Chronic anger and dissatisfaction

Would leaders rather have employees distracted and confused by leadership process errors, or instead engaged and focused on both doing and improving their work?

While the number of people affected and the extent to which they are affected varies, these outcomes must be seen by leaders as abnormal conditions that are both undesirable and avoidable. Fundamentally, it is not the job of leaders to create human health problems or cause human suffering. Organizations need more than leaders who are little more than task-masters and budget-cutters whose work gives the appearance of getting things done. They need in each leader the ability to think and do; people who think about the consequences associated with what they do and how they do it.

Organizations need professional, not amateur leaders.

This chapter makes clear the negative effects that leadership process errors have on employee health and work activities. These bad outcomes help you understand why respecting people is fundamental and required in any effort to improve processes. Its absence in traditional batch-and-queue management compounds information flow problems. Leaders should always be attentive to the social and psychological stress that business targets, performance reviews, performance metrics, etc., create in organizations.

Remember, blocked information flow is the silent killer of organizations. It is slow, relentless organizational suicide. Leaders who refuse to improve leadership process are organizationally suicidal and therefore remiss in their core responsibility of ensuring the long-term survival of the organization. This undercuts both fiduciary duty and moral duty.

If it is not already obvious, there is a very important connection to recognize:

Bad leadership processes create bad leadership behaviors.

And, in the case of psychopaths, bad leadership behaviors annihilate good leadership processes and also cause human health problems and human suffering.

Included in this is organizational politics, which simply adds cost and creates no value. It leads to massive delays and extensive re-work. Typically, leaders selfishly use organizational politics to normalize chaos rather than work to reduce or eliminate the chaos at its source. Why is there chaos? It is because leadership processes are poor, error-ridden, and vary widely from one leader to another.

For these reasons, leadership processes must be improved.

Questions For The Executive Team

Some important questions emerge from Chapter 3:

- What are the top 5 mental effects that our leadership has on employees?
- What are the top 5 physical effects that our leadership has on employees?
- What are the top 5 work-related effects that our leadership has on employees?
- What has been our idea of good leadership?
- Why do we think that is good leadership?
- Why has our idea of leadership not resulted in better leadership?
- Why do we tolerate bad leadership?
- Why do we accept leadership process variation?
- Why have we been willing to accept leadership process errors and their financial and non-financial consequences?
- Why do we treat symptoms instead of correcting the root cause of problems?

A wise man once said:

The employees are offering a very important part of their life to us. If we don't use their time effectively, we are wasting their lives.

- Have we been wasting employees' lives? Why?
- Is it within the scope of leadership responsibility to waste employees' lives?
- How can we use employees' time more effectively?
- What can we do to reduce or eliminate this problem?

Discuss these questions as a senior management team. Use structured problem-solving processes to answer these questions and provide direction for improvement. Summarize the results of the discussion and problem-solving in two or three flip-chart pages, and post them on a wall for further thought and analysis.

Thoughts, Observations, and Actions To Take

Thoughts, Observations, and Actions To Take

4

Rightsizing Leadership

As businesses grow, their processes become bigger, more complicated, with many more steps, and which therefore requires greater human skill. To cope with this, managers hire more people with greater levels of formal education that cost more in salary and benefits order to manage the complexity, and who invariably make the work even more complex over time. Managers also purchase bigger and more expensive equipment, which promotes batch-and-queue processing and overproduction, and creates bottlenecks, quality problems, and long lead-times.

The equipment purchased is typically multi-functional in the hope of generating various benefits, including economies of scale, while usually ignoring various other costs as well as diseconomies of scale. By not understanding the function of the process in relation to the need of the product or service, processes become very complicated. Without realizing it, managers inadvertently increase both operating costs and labor costs, and reduce the organization's flexibility and responsiveness to changing conditions.

Occasionally, the leaders of a company will recognize the unfavorable impact that big and complicated equipment has on their costs and their ability to satisfy customers. So, they will go down the path of "rightsizing" the equipment. What does that mean? And what are the effects on the business and its customers?

Rightsizing is a term that originated in manufacturing, and we will use this framework to explain the concept. Rightsizing means to use inexpensive equipment whose size is proportional to the part being made, and which performs a single function. Rightsizing equipment offers numerous benefits including: continuous flow of material (parts), fewer defects, shorter lead-times, and lower operating costs – both for equipment and because high quality work can be performed with lower levels of skill.

In order to right-size equipment, the function of the equipment in relation to the part being produced must be understood. Parts often require many different manufacturing processes to move from raw material to finished good. But, there is no rule in manufacturing that says many processes must be performed on a single piece of equipment. The same is true for service processes.

The table below shows various manufacturing processes and the function of each process.

Manufacturing Process	Function
Weld	Join Pieces
Drill	Make Hole
Turn	Reduce Diameter
Mill	Change Shape
Wash	Clean
Gage Check	Measure Dimension
Heat Treat	Change Properties
Press	Stamp / Bend / Cut
Forge	Change Shape / Work Harden
Cast	Create Shape
Saw	Cut
Paint	Add Polymer Coating(s)
Form / Bend	Create / Change Shape
Grind	Reduce Diameter
Electroplate	Add Layer(s) of Metal

Can you think of analogues for service processes and their corresponding functions?

In looking at the table above, ask yourself: "What is the context for each manufacturing process and function?" Is it for the process to be performed *incorrectly*? No, the context is for the process and function to be performed correctly – every time, and not just once in a while.

Next, ask yourself: "What is important to the part?" Is it the size of equipment? No. The make of the equipment? No. The model of the equipment? No. The country of origin? No. None of that matters to the part. The only thing that matters is that the manufacturing process performs the corresponding function correctly.

Let's carry this concept of "rightsizing" equipment over to the realm of leadership.

Have leadership processes become too big and complicated? Has it resulted in batch-and-queue processing, overproduction, bottlenecks, quality problems, and long lead-times? Has the efficiency of leadership been reduced by its complexity? Is the cost too high in relationship to the service performed?

Leadership can become too big and complicated by various means, most of which likely have good intentions: one's own doing, corporate mandates, academic research, trainers and consultants seeking to provide a better service, and so on. Irrespective of the means or intentions, complicated leadership models and practices can propel leaders to instead focus on self-interest. While this is easier for them, it is worse for other people.

Evidence that big and complicated leadership exists in your organizations is when people (followers and others) recognize that it's all about "me," the leader, not about "you," the employee or the customer.

Leaders who are more interested in serving themselves than they are of serving others will make life very difficult for employees, as well as customers and suppliers. Aggrandizement of one's self usually comes at the expense of others. The true function of leadership and of each leadership process has been lost.

The table below shows the function of leadership when each leadership processes becomes self-serving. The definition of "leadership" as one who leads people no longer applies. While the person may be in a leadership position, they are not leading people. Instead, they are leading only themselves. And to a destination they probably do not even know.

Leadership Process	Function
1. Leading and Managing People	Generate Fear and Intimidation; Coerce People
2. Planning and Budgeting	All Upside, Downside Risks Ignored
3. Workload Management	Overload People With Work
4. Decision-Making	Ad Hoc, Delay, Avoid
5. Problem Recognition and Response	Ignore Problems
6. Problem-Solving	Ad Hoc
7. Management Reviews (finance, operations, HR, etc.)	Belittle and Berate People
8. Employee Feedback and Coaching	Belittle and Berate People
9. Team Meetings	Reinforce Leader's Agenda
10. Asking Questions, Listening, and Receiving Feedback	Avoid, Ignore
11. Information Sharing	Withhold Information; Knowledge is Power
12. Developing People	Avoid, Ignore
13. Performance Appraisal	Belittle and Berate People
14. Walking Around, "Go See"	Stay in Office; Associate with Peers and Boss
15. Stakeholder Engagement (customers, suppliers, investors, communities)	Avoid, Ignore

Rightsizing leadership means to perform only the necessary function for each of the 15 leadership processes, to improve information flow and assure error-free results in interactions with employees and other stakeholders.

The next page contains a table listing the 15 leadership processes and corresponding function. Fill in the "Function" column. Think deeply about the basic function of each leadership process. It should be simple, concise, and accurate, in as few words as possible, and not a laundry list of things. The function should, of course, be "them-focused," not "me-focused." After you have spent some time filling in the "Function" column in the above table, compare your inputs to those on the page below.

Remember to ask yourself: "What is the context for each leadership process and function?" Is it for the process to be performed *incorrectly*? No, the context is for the process and function to be performed correctly – every time, and not just once in a while.

Next, ask yourself: "What is important to the employee?" Is it the size of leader's department? No. The leader's resume? No. The leader's degrees? No. The leader's alma mater? No. None of that matters to the employee (or supplier, or customer, or investor, or community). The only thing that matters is that the leadership process performs the corresponding function correctly.

Leadership Process	Function
1. Leading and Managing People	
2. Planning and Budgeting	
3. Workload Management	
4. Decision-Making	
5. Problem Recognition and Response	
6. Problem-Solving	
7. Management Reviews (finance, operations, HR, etc.)	
8. Employee Feedback and Coaching	
9. Team Meetings	
10. Asking Questions, Listening, and Receiving Feedback	
11. Information Sharing	
12. Developing People	
13. Performance Appraisal	
14. Walking Around, "Go See"	
15. Stakeholder Engagement (customers, suppliers, investors, communities)	

Leadership Process	Function
1. Leading and Managing People	Guidance and Teaching
2. Planning and Budgeting	Allocate Resources
3. Workload Management	Allocate Work
4. Decision-Making	Select Course or Action
5. Problem Recognition and Response	Awareness In-Time and Take Action
6. Problem-Solving	Identify Cause and Implement Countermeasure, or Solution
7. Management Reviews (finance, operations, HR, etc.)	Engagement, Awareness, and Improvement
8. Employee Feedback and Coaching	Teaching, Learning, Improvement
9. Team Meetings	Communicate Current and Future State
10. Asking Questions, Listening, and Receiving Feedback	Engagement, Awareness, and Improvement
11. Information Sharing	Communicate In-Time
12. Developing People	Improve Current Skills or Learn New Skills (Learning)
13. Performance Appraisal	Teaching, Learning, Improvement
14. Walking Around, "Go See"	Engagement, Awareness, and Improvement
15. Stakeholder Engagement (customers, suppliers, investors, communities)	Engagement, Awareness, and Improvement

Each of the functions shown above are examples, not necessarily answers. They are a guide and will hopefully inspire you think for yourself.

Please remember the context for the above processes and functions: performed correctly – every time, to the greatest extent possible, and not just once in a while. And remember, "What is important to the employee?" What matters to employees is that the leadership process performs the corresponding function correctly.

Rightsizing leadership will make leadership less complicated. It will enlarge the pool of people in your organization who can become capable leaders. It will result in a continuous flow of information, fewer defects, fewer delays, and shorter lead-times. It will lower operating costs in two ways: more timely processing of information (where time is money), and avoid costly problems (product defects and recalls, service delivery failures, damaged corporate reputation, etc.) that inevitably result from blocked information flows.

There is one final thing to consider: Inspections

Let's return to the manufacturing example. Parts are inspected in manufacturing processes, typically in batches (especially when big, complicated equipment is used), which causes delays in the delivery of goods to customers. Rightsizing equipment also means to right-size inspection processes within or between steps in the manufacturing process. Instead of using expensive computerized machines that take a long time (several minutes to hours) to inspect each part, simple, inexpensive gages are used, with each inspection taking only one or two seconds.

As a leader, you must also right-size your processes for inspecting and approving employees' work. Leaders must not become the bottleneck in workflows because this increases lead-times and does not respect employees or customers.

How can you improve your inspection processes within and between the steps in employees' work processes so that it takes only one or two seconds, or one or two minutes? Don't you think employees will like quick management inspections better than protracted and labored management inspections?

Questions For The Executive Team

Some important questions emerge from Chapter 4:

- Why do we succumb to complexity when it comes to leadership? What is the allure of complex leadership models and practices?

- What is the mechanism by which leadership becomes all about "me" instead of being about "them?" How do we prevent that from happening?

- When leadership is all about "me," aren't we more likely to ignore information, base decisions on beliefs instead of facts, and crush dissent? Don't we get away with doing this all the time and ignore the danger it represents to employees, suppliers, investors, and the company itself? That's scary!

- We have been leaders for a long time; how could we not have seen this? Have we been blinded by our success, and not recognized how big and complicated leadership leads us towards self-interest and failure?

- Why do we not understand the function of leadership since it is so important to our success?

- Employees do not want big and complicated leadership. Why do we do that? It makes our job harder for no reason.

- Won't we perform better and also feel better if we right-size leadership? It will reduce our stress and employees' stress. It's a healthier way to lead.

Discuss these questions as a senior management team. Use structured problem-solving processes to answer these questions and provide direction for improvement. Summarize the results of the discussion and problem-solving in two or three flip-chart pages, and post them on a wall for further thought and analysis.

Thoughts, Observations, and Actions To Take

Thoughts, Observations, and Actions To Take

5

Standards For Leadership Processes

Standards can be found in all types of work and activities. In sports, standards exist for training and in the form of records (time or quantity) that top athletes have achieved. In the industries such as automotive, aerospace, food (human, dog, cat, bird), construction, and pharmaceuticals, rigorous standards exist to assure quality, and safety, and that products and services meet customer's needs and expectations. Standards exist in service industries such as healthcare, restaurant, fast food, hotel, airlines, higher education, and insurance.

Standards are ubiquitous. Yet, when it comes to leadership, clear and objective standards do not exist. It is an "I know it when I see it" thing. But, that hazy, weak standard is subjective and prone to bias. Jack Welch, the former CEO of General Electric, is seen by some as a great leader, and by others as a terrible leader. The same will no doubt be the case for his successor, Jeffrey Immelt.

Leaders within the same company may be free to lead in any way they like, ranging from servant leader to psychopath. There is no reference point, no explicit standard, so we cannot know for certain if our leader is good, bad, or just eccentric. In other cases, leaders may not be free to lead as they wish, but instead are guided to lead as the boss does. The current boss may be a tyrant, someday to be replaced by a benevolent leader. In still other cases, there may be an explicit standard, but it is likely to be generic and subject to wide interpretation. Some leaders will model themselves after the standard while others will not. The existence of standards demand accountability, in a non-blaming and non-judgmental way, and do not permit freedom to do as one chooses simply because one is a leader.

The same is true for leadership processes. In the absence of standards, we cannot know for certain if a problem exists in a leadership process. Leaders do not know whether the situation is normal or abnormal. As a result, leadership suffers from enormous variation. Standards for each process must be established as the basis for which leadership processes can be improved. This is likely something that you have never thought of doing. Why have you never thought to do this?

Your challenge in the coming pages is to create standards for each of the 15 leadership processes. Do not try to create the perfect standard. Just create something that is much better than exists today, but which is still within reach. Be aggressive because often a standard that appears to be an ideal condition turns out to be practical and achievable – the normal condition – with focused effort over a period of time.

Creating standards for each of the 15 leadership processes is much more than just an exercise. Creating standards for each process puts you on a path forward from amateur to professional leader – one who makes few mistakes. But, when mistakes are made, they no longer have large negative impact on employees, suppliers, customers, or investors.

Standards provide you with tangible goals that you will achieve, step-by-step, through the elimination of leadership process errors. You will learn how to do this in Chapter 6.

In the coming 15 pages, please create a standard for each leadership process (the normal condition). You can do this individually or as a senior management team. Do not rush; think slowly and carefully, and proceed with this in mind:

> Leadership process errors are abnormal conditions that prevent the 15 processes from getting close to the standard. What is the standard (target) condition for each leadership process?

Revise and edit your input as needed, but do not spend weeks doing this. Otherwise, you will never make it to the next step of establishing and improving leadership processes.

Worksheet 1

Standard for Leading and Managing People

Worksheet 2

Standard for Planning and Budgeting

Worksheet 3

Standard for Workload Management

Worksheet 4

Standard for Decision-Making

Worksheet 5

Standard for Problem Recognition and Response

Worksheet 6

Standard for Problem-Solving

Worksheet 7

Standard for Management Reviews

Worksheet 8

Standard for Employee Feedback and Coaching

Worksheet 9

Standard for Team Meetings

Worksheet 10

Standard for Asking Questions, Listening, and Receiving Feedback

Worksheet 11

Standard for Information Sharing

Worksheet 12

Standard for Developing People

Worksheet 13

Standard for Performance Appraisal

Worksheet 14

Standard for Walk Around, Go See

Worksheet 15

Standard for Stakeholder Engagement

Turn the page only after you have written down standards for each of the 15 leadership processes.

Review the table below and compare your ideas for standards for leadership processes to these:

Standards for Leadership Processes	
Leadership Process	**Standard (Target) Condition**
1. Leading and Managing People	Respect people. No blame. Problems are good. Flow. Helpful and motivating. Trained and coached in leadership processes.
2. Planning and Budgeting	Quarterly, Fact-based and reality-based. Quick and easy.
3. Workload Management	Leveled work. Task matches skill. Clear responsibilities and expectations.
4. Decision-Making	Timely. Fact-based. No illogical thinking. No decision-making traps. Accept input from others.
5. Problem Recognition and Response	Abnormal conditions indicated by visual controls. Standard response. Quick response.
6. Problem-Solving	Everyone uses same problem-solving methods (top-to-bottom). Quick. Focus on actual root cause(s). Thoughtfully evaluate alternatives and consequences.
7. Management Reviews	Clear expectations, helpful, fact-based, improvement-focused. No blame.
8. Employee Feedback and Coaching	Daily, fact-based, constructive. Emphasize the positive.
9. Team Meetings	Quick. Right information, right amount, right time. Start and end on time. Follow-up is on-time and done right.
10. Asking Questions, Listening, and Receiving Feedback	Daily. Ask meaningful questions. Active listening. No fear of reprisal. Positive response to feedback. Action taken based on feedback.
11. Information Sharing	Timely Sharing. Quick. No batching of information. No spin.
12. Developing People	Daily. Specific and actionable feedback (1 to 3 items). Generous with training opportunities (OJT, cross-training, and formal).
13. Performance Appraisal	Quarterly, quick, accurate, and on-time. Positive focus on improvement.
14. Walking Around, "Go See"	Knowledge of process. Daily. Ask meaningful questions. Observe. Learn from others. Help others improve.
15. Stakeholder Engagement	Understands expectations. Timely, collaborative, non-zero-sum. Joint problem-solving. Responsive.

Notice that some of the standards are unchanging over time and achievable, while others require the creation of standard work that will change over time.

Finally, my best teachers never gave me answers. They guided me towards answers. The result was more effective learning. Likewise, the standards shown in the table above are examples meant to guide you towards your own answers. Think for yourself.

Questions For The Executive Team

Some important questions emerge from Chapter 5:

- Why have we not thought about standards for leadership processes?
- What have been the consequence of our past efforts to improve leadership without standards?
- Why do we accept abnormal conditions as normal? How does that acceptance affect the ways in which we lead? How does that affect employees and other stakeholders?
- What process can we use to reach consensus on standards for each of the 15 leadership processes?
- How do documents that appear to function as standards (e.g. Code of Ethics) relate to the 15 leadership processes? Do they support or contradict one another? How do we illustrate connections between the leadership process standards and our Code of Ethics document?
- How do we visually communicate standards for the 15 leadership processes to employees?

Discuss these questions as a senior management team. Use structured problem-solving processes to answer these questions and provide direction for improvement. Summarize the results of the discussion and problem-solving in two or three flip-chart pages, and post them on a wall for further thought and analysis.

Thoughts, Observations, and Actions To Take

Thoughts, Observations, and Actions To Take

6

Improving Leadership Processes

Because leadership is an observable phenomenon, it can be studied using the Scientific Method. Leadership is subject to cause-and-effect, which means that leadership problems can be understood and corrected using root cause analysis (5 Whys and fishbone diagram) and related structured problem-solving methods such as Plan-Do-Check-Act (PDCA) cycle or A3 reports. This makes leadership more science than art. You may need to perform formal root cause analysis on some leadership problems as part of your effort to improve leadership processes.

The process perspective of leadership is practical, objective, and fact-based. It has distinct advantages in that it is more effective in helping to comprehend leadership and factually distinguish between good and bad leadership. It helps us recognize that leadership is not the domain of a few people who possess unique personal characteristics such as charisma or authenticity. Understanding leadership as processes and recognizing leadership process errors means that anyone can improve their leadership skills and capabilities.

The process perspective also helps us better evaluate leadership capabilities and effectiveness. It enables us to recognize the variation in how each leader operates processes that are common among them. Note that a leadership team would be intolerant of a work team where each individual or team operated the process differently. Yet, in most organizations, there is no requirement placed on a leadership team to operate its common processes with little variation.

The leadership variation that employee's experience, shown in Chapter 2, is dramatic and contributes greatly to perceptions of poor leadership. This makes it difficult for employees to do their jobs and is a great source of daily frustration. In addition, if the quality of each of the 15 leadership processes is chronically low, then acute circumstances requiring intelligent, accurate, and decisive leadership are likely to be absent.

Leaders need followers to get things done. Followers need leaders to know what to do and by when to do it. The work of leaders precedes that of followers, so the direction set by leaders must be precise and not result in confusion or re-work for followers.

Improvement cannot be without purpose. The tangible and reachable goal of improving leadership processes must be connected to the organization's needs and goals in relation to customer's interests. Leadership process improvement is informed by practical needs and goals such as these:

- Improve the value proposition for customers
- Reduce costs
- Increase profits
- Grow market share

Focus on process, which will then yield the desired result. The process perspective of leadership leads one to think about how to improve leadership processes and then how make the improved process the standard by which leaders do their work.

Do not let the number of errors within each process or in total, as shown in Chapter 2, deter you. If you look carefully, you will realize there is a hierarchy of errors within each category. That means if you eliminate 3 or 4 of the right errors, you may eliminate the remaining 10 to 20 errors within that category.

There are two practical ways of improving leadership processes. The first is to create simple visuals that remind leaders of what to do or what not to do. These should be sketches that contain signs, symbols, emojis, and other information that convey specific errors to avoid in each one of the 15 leadership processes. Leaders can create these individually, or as a team. The idea is to create a small number of highly effective visuals that all leaders will use to improve the common processes that they are engaged in.

The visuals should be hand-drawn, preferably using colored pens or markers. There is no need to spend time or money to create professional illustrations. The visuals are not meant to last a lifetime. They are mean only to last until someone thinks up of a more effective visual. That could be one day or a few weeks, but not months or years. The latter would indicate that leaders are not thinking; that they are instead rote following the visual. These visuals should be posted in leaders' work areas to remind them of leadership process errors to avoid. It is a form of daily training for leadership development.

The image on the following page shows a format to create simple but effective visuals. Use it as follows:

Step 1: Begin by filling out the "Prepared by box."

Step 2: Next, refer to the leadership processes in Chapter 2. Start with the first leadership process: "Leading and Managing People." Circle the number 1 in the box labeled "Leadership Process impacted." It is possible that more than one leadership process could be circles, but never more than two or three.

Step 3: Refer again to the leadership process errors for "Leading and Managing People" in Chapter 2. Identify two or three leadership process errors that cause employees a lot of trouble. Next, write the leadership processes errors that you intend to eliminate by using the visual.

Step 4: Create the visual. It could be a single image or a "before" image on the left side and an "after" image on the right side to denote abnormal and normal conditions.

Step 5: Fill in the box "Explain how leaders should use this visual."

Step 6: Create three or four visual concepts and decide as a team which visual is most helpful.

This should be a fun activity. Improvement must be fun, otherwise people, leaders included, will not do it.

Leadership Process Visual	Explain how leaders should use this visual:	Prepared by:	Leadership Process Impacted	Leadership Process Errors Eliminated (minimum of one)
			1 2 3 4 5	•
			6 7 8 9 10	•
			11 12 13 14 15	•

The following pages show examples of visuals that convey information about specific errors to avoid in various leadership processes. These examples are not answers. They are a few of many, many possibilities. Think for yourself.

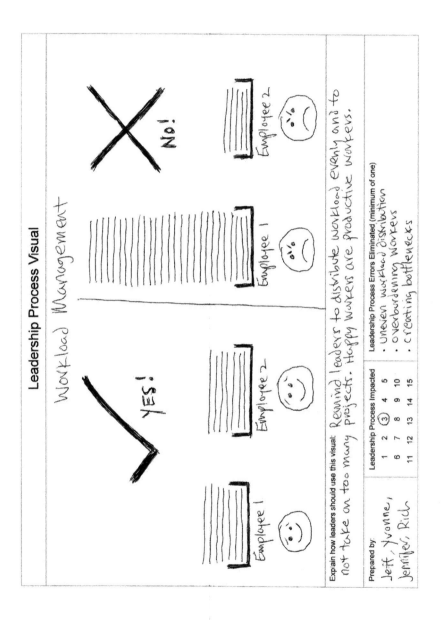

Leadership Process Visual

Workload Management

No!

Yes!

Employee 1   Employee 2   Employee 1   Employee 2

Explain how leaders should use this visual: Remind leaders to distribute workload evenly and to not take on too many projects. Happy workers are productive workers.

Prepared by:
Jeff, Yvonne, Jennifer, Rich

Leadership Process Impacted

1	2	③	4	5
6	7	8	9	10
11	12	13	14	15

Leadership Process Errors Eliminated (minimum of one)
- Uneven workload distribution
- overburdening workers
- creating bottlenecks

Leadership Process Visual

Asking Questions, Listening, Receiving Feedback / Problem Recognition & Response / Walking Around, "Go See"

What Problems Are You Experiencing Today?

How Can I Help You Improve the Process?

Lapel Badge
(similar to name tag)

Explain how leaders should use this visual: Leader wears badge on daily walk-arounds. Leader carries pen and paper to take notes. This engages leader in daily problems to understand actual conditions.

Leadership Process Impacted

1	2	3	4	⑤
6	7	8	9	⑩
11	12	13	⑭	15

Leadership Process Errors Eliminated (minimum of one)
- Disinterest in problems / disinterest in processes
- Not asking questions
- Employees concerns ignored

Prepared by: Mark, Sheila, Roy

Leadership Process Visual

Developing People

1   2   3

Explain how leaders should use this visual: 1. Employee needs development. 2. Employee is developing 3. Employee developed. Use to remind leaders of their daily responsibility to personally develop employees and provide training and career development opportunities.

Prepared by:
Shondra, Will, Tracy, Maria

Leadership Process Impacted

1	2	3	4	5
6	7	8	9	10
11	(12)	13	14	15

Leadership Process Errors Eliminated (minimum of one)
- Does not develop people
- Denies training or development opportunities
- Develops only favorite people

Leadership Process Visual

Decision - Making

Decision-Making Traps

☐ Anchoring
☐ Status-Quo
☐ Sunk Cost
☐ Confirming Evidence
☐ Framing
☐ Estimating/Forecasting

Illogical Thinking

☐ Denying the Antecedent
☐ False Assumption
☐ Using & Abusing Tradition
☐ Ad Hominem
☐ Avoiding the Force of Reason
☐ Abuse of Expertise
☐ Red Herring
☐ Inability to Disprove Does Not Prove
☐ False Dilemma
☐ Special Pleading
☐ Expediency

Explain how leaders should use this visual: Leadership team & individual leaders use as a checklist to avoid making bad decisions.

Prepared by:	Leadership Process Impacted					Leadership Process Errors Eliminated (minimum of one)
Raul, Vanessa	1	2	3	④	5	• Ignoring information
Tim	6	7	8	9	10	• Jumping to conclusions/solutions
	11	12	13	14	15	• Not exploring alternatives

Use visuals in combination with the second method to improve leadership processes, which is a bit more challenging. Call it "standard work." In this context, "standard work" describes the way the leadership process is to be performed until such time as improvements are made based on new ideas and new circumstances. Therefore, it is critically important to understand that standard work is *not* the one best way. It is merely the current way of doing the work in never-ending cycles of continuous improvement (i.e. PDCA) that occur frequently over time.

Creating standard work for leadership processes establishes the standard upon which continuous improvement is made. Rather than doing bad work slowly, improvement must result in good work done quickly and repeatably – meaning, absence of queue time, but *not* speeding people up; neither leader nor worker.

Standard work is documented in a simple one-page chart that can be easily understood at a glance. The standard work chart is a description of the new process in the form of a checklist, sketch, or both. However the work is described, it should fit on one page and inform people what the process is and the steps performed by the leader to complete the process.

The following three pages show leadership process standard work forms for three elements of work:

- Preparation
- Execution
- Follow-up

The first chart shows preparation, the second execution, and the third follow-up. Standard work charts are created for all three parts of a leadership process; in this example, Workload Management, which is one of the primary concerns of workers.

The frequency of a leadership process such as Workload Management depends upon various factors and includes considerations of the needs of employees. Generally, the frequency of a leadership process such as Workload Management should be daily or a few times a day, depending upon needs, but could be weekly.

Standard Work Sheet

| Leader/Dept: | Scope of Process | From: Preparation | Date: |
| | | To: Execution | Revision: 01 |

Leadership Process: Workload Mgmt Preparation

List the major steps in the process or create a checklist.

Notes or simple sketch of the major steps (work) to be performed.

1. ☐
2. ☐
3. ☐
4. ☐
5. ☐
6. ☐
7. ☐
8. ☐
9. ☐

| Quality Check ◇ | Precaution ✛ | Cycle Time   sec | Lship Process Errors Affected |

Standard Work Sheet

Leader/Dept:		Scope of Process	From: Execution	Date:
Leadership Process: Workload Mgmt Execution			To: Follow-Up	Revision: 01

List the major steps in the process or create a checklist.

Notes or simple sketch of the major steps (work) to be performed.

1. ☐

2. ☐

3. ☐

4. ☐

5. ☐

6. ☐

7. ☐

8. ☐

9. ☐

Quality Check ◇	Precaution ✚	Cycle Time sec	Lship Process Errors Affected

Standard Work Sheet

Leader/Dept:	Scope of Process	From: Follow-Up	Date:
Leadership Process: Workload Mgmt Follow-Up		To: Preparation	Revision: 01

List the major steps in the process or create a checklist.

Notes or simple sketch of the major steps (work) to be performed.

1. _____ ☐
2. _____ ☐
3. _____ ☐
4. _____ ☐
5. _____ ☐
6. _____ ☐
7. _____ ☐
8. _____ ☐
9. _____ ☐

| Quality Check ◇ | Precaution ✚ | Cycle Time | sec | Lship Process Errors Affected |

Next comes the creation of more detailed descriptions of the work. This is called a "Standard Work Combination Sheet" (SWCS), as shown on the following page. The word "combination" refers to the combination of discrete activities that comprise the work to be performed. The upper right corner shows the symbolic notation used to describe the various activities that make up leadership work:

- Manual processing
- Talking
- Listening
- Thinking / Observing
- Walking
- Waiting
- Automatic (machine processing)

Manual processing is an activity such as writing e-mails or creating spreadsheets. Talking, listening, thinking / observing, walking, and waiting are self-explanatory. In most cases, automatic means where a leader is using a machine to do work, such as sending an e-mail or perform a calculation. In most cases, the automatic time is short, a few seconds, compared to a worker on the shop or office floor where automatic time may be several minutes or more.

The following three pages show leadership processes standard work combination sheets for three elements of work:

- Preparation
- Execution
- Follow-up

For both standard work and standard work combination sheets, preparation prior to execution is critically important, because it is the part of the work where leaders often fail. How often have you joined a team meeting late and were unprepared? The lack of preparation likely resulted in poor execution. Workers notice this and judge their leaders to lacking in both capability and credibility.

Standard Work Combination Sheet		Prepared By:		Manual (M)
Leadership Process: Workload Mgmt Preparation		Date:		Talk (T)
				Listen (L)
				Think /Obs (O)
				Walking (K)
				Wait (W)
				Automatic (A)

Work Sequence — Page 1 of 1 — Frequency: Once per day — Cycle Time: 660 sec (11 min)

Time, seconds

Step	Description of Activity	Time						
		M	T	L	T/O	K	W	A

TOTALS

LPEs Eliminated:

Standard Work Combination Sheet

Leadership Process: Workload Mgmt Execution

Prepared By:

Date:

Cycle Time: 240 sec (4 min)

Work Sequence	Page 1 of 1	Frequency: Once per day

Manual (M)
Talk (T)
Listen (L)
Think / Obs (O)
Walking (K)
Wait (W)
Automatic (A)

Step	Description of Activity	M	T	L	T/O	K	W	A	Time, seconds

CT

Time, seconds: 100 200 300 400 500 600 700 800 900 1000 1100 1200 1300

TOTALS

LPEs Eliminated:

Standard Work Combination Sheet

Leadership Process: Workload Mgmt Follow-Up

Work Sequence — Page 1 of 1

Prepared By:

Date:

Frequency: Once per day

Cycle Time: 1140 sec (18 min)

Legend:
- Manual (M) — ////////////
- Talk (T) — ▓▓▓▓▓
- Listen (L)
- Think/Obs (O) — ooooooooooo
- Walking (K) — ᴧᴧᴧᴧᴧᴧᴧᴧ
- Wait (W) — ↕
- Automatic (A)

Time, seconds: 100 200 300 400 500 600 700 800 900 1000 1100 1200 1300   CT

Step	Description of Activity	M	T	L	T/O	K	W	A
TOTALS								

LPEs Eliminated:

The standard work combination sheet is completed by breaking down the work process into its component steps (Work Sequence), which is taken from the standard work chart shown previously. The time it takes to perform each step is determined using a stopwatch. Yes, a stopwatch; exact times are needed, not estimates. Time must be measured in seconds, not minutes, and definitely not hours.

Next, a horizontal line is drawn to express the duration of each step using the legend shown in the upper right corner. Add up the totals for the time it takes to perform each element of work. The bottom right portion of the SWCS form says "LPEs Eliminated." This is the place to document the leadership process errors (Chapter 2) that have been eliminated as a result of creating and using the standard work combination sheet.

Please remember that improving a leadership process means to simultaneously shorten the cycle time, reduce the lead-time, improve quality (reduce errors), reduce cost, and improve employee satisfaction. The charts in the three previous pages show a solid vertical line "CT" (drawn in red), which is an assumed cycle time for preparation, execution, and follow-up. Your actual cycle times, measured using a stopwatch, will be different.

You will struggle a bit to create standard work charts and standard work combination sheets because you are not familiar with this way of thinking. And, you will quickly realize that creating standard work charts and standard work combination sheets is more difficult than it looks. But, you will succeed.

Leaders who perform the 15 leadership processes according to standard work charts and standard work combination sheets will be praised for their understanding of the process and error-free execution. If errors are made, then standard work needs to be corrected and revised.

The following pages show examples of standard work charts and standard work combination sheets for the leadership process Team Meetings (Preparation, Execution, Follow-Up). These examples are not answers. They are a few of many, many possibilities, depending on your processes. You must create these standard work charts and standard work combination sheets yourself, making errors along the way that will help you learn so you can teach this method to future leaders. Think for yourself.

Standard Work Sheet

Leader/Dept: Asif / Finance	Scope of	From: Preparation	Date: 8 June 2015
Leadership Process: Team Meeting Preparation	Process #9	To: Execution	Revision: 01

List the major steps in the process or create a checklist. | Notes or simple sketch of the major steps (work) to be performed.

1. Review previous team meeting minutes ☐
2. Review metrics & related facts/info ☐
3. Obtain supplemental information ☐
4. Edit agenda notes & sub-topics ✚ ◇
5. Print agenda and related handouts ☐
6. Walk to printer to collect printout ☐
7. Inspect Printout ◇
8. Walk back to desk ☐
9. _____ ☐

Notes

Use standard structured agenda format

Write brief narrative to quickly convey facts in writing vs. speaking

Quality Check ◇	Precaution ✚	Cycle Time 965 sec	Lship Process Errors Affected	No agenda, meeting goes off-topic, missing meeting materials

Standard Work Combination Sheet

Prepared By: Asif

Leadership Process: Team Meeting Preparation   #9

Date: 8 June 2015

Page 1 of 1

Frequency: Once per day

Cycle Time: 985 Sec

Legend:
- ||||||||||| Manual (M)
- ——— Talk (T)
- ooooooooooo Listen (L)
- ooooooooo Think /Obs (O)
- WWWWWWW Walking (K)
- ↕ Wait (W)
- ----- Automatic (A)

Step	Description of Activity	M	T	L	T/O	K	W	A
1	Review previous team meeting minutes				65			
2	Review metrics and related facts/info				194			
3	Obtain supplemental information			138	310			
4	Edit agenda notes and sub-topics			222				
5	Print agenda & related handouts							27
6	Walk to printer to collect printout				24			
7	Inspect printout			25				
8	Walk back to desk				24			

TOTALS 222 138 310 284 47

[7] LPEs Eliminated: No agenda, Mtg goes off topic, missing meeting materials

Time, seconds (100 200 300 400 500 600 700 800 900 1000 1100 1200 1300)

CT

Standard Work Sheet

Leader/Dept: Asif / Finance	Scope of	From: Execution	Date: 8 June 2015
Leadership Process: Team Meeting Execution	Process #9	To: Follow-Up	Revision: 01

List the major steps in the process or create a checklist.

	Step	Notes or simple sketch of the major steps (work) to be performed.
1.	Collect meeting Materials ✚ ☐	Notes
2.	Walk to Conference room 3 ☐	3 standard agenda items per daily meeting
3.	Opening remarks ☐	
4.	Discuss Standard agenda item 1 ☐	15 total standard agenda items per week
5.	Record outcomes ◇ ☐	
6.	Discuss Standard agenda item 2 ☐	Focus/simplify agenda items to reduce processing time.
7.	Record outcomes ◇ ☐	
8.	Discuss Standard agenda item 3 ☐	
9.	Record outcomes ◇ ☐	
10.	closing remarks ✚	
11.	Walk back to office	

| Quality Check ◇ | Precaution ✚ | Cycle Time 9147 sec | Lship Process Errors Affected | Meeting runs long; not listening to employees, meeting goes off topic |

Standard Work Combination Sheet

Prepared By: Asif

Leadership Process: Team Meeting Execution   #9

Date: 8 June 2015

Page 1 of 1

Frequency: Once per day

Cycle Time: 947 sec.

Legend:
- Manual (M) ——————
- Talk (T) ////////
- Listen (L) oooooooooo
- Think /Obs (O)
- Walking (W) wwwww
- Wait (W) (arrows)
- Automatic (A) - - - - -
- CT

Step	Description of Activity	M	T	L	T/O	K	W	A
1	Collect meeting materials	39						
2	Walk to conference room 3					51		
3	Opening remarks		60					
4	Discuss standard agenda item 1		9	180				
5	Record outcomes	35						
6	Discuss standard agenda item 2		9	180				
7	Record outcomes	35						
8	Discuss standard agenda item 3		9	180				
9	Record outcomes	35						
10	Closing remarks		28					
11	Walk back to office					51		
TOTALS		142	115	540		102		

Time, seconds — 100 200 300 400 500 600 700 800 900 1000 1100 1200 1300

LPEs Eliminated: Meeting runs long, not listening, meeting goes off topic

Standard Work Sheet

Leader/Dept: Asif / Finance		Scope of Process	From: Follow-Up	Date: 8 June 2015
Leadership Process: Team Meeting Follow-Up		#5	To: Preparation	Revision: 01

List the major steps in the process or create a checklist. | Notes or simple sketch of the major steps (work) to be performed.

1. Review team meeting minutes ☐
2. Identify action items for self and schedule completion ☐
3. Follow-up with team members who have been assigned action items ☐
4. Follow-up with others who have been assigned action items ☐
5. Update visual board ◇
6. _____ ☐
7. _____ ☐
8. _____ ☐
9. _____ ☐

Notes:

Be careful not to generate leadership process errors caused by careless or disrespectful follow-up.

| Quality Check ◇ | Precaution ✛ | Cycle Time 738 sec | Lship Process Errors Affected | No follow-up; action items not completed on-time. |

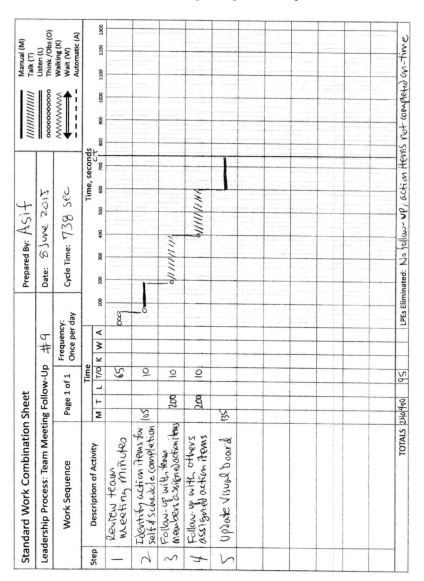

The ability to create standard work and standard work combination sheets will demonstrate to others that you possess a strong understanding of your leadership processes. It also forces leaders to think critically about the steps in each of their processes and how long each step really takes, as measured by a stopwatch. It is only with this level of detail can leaders say they truly know their processes.

With practice, you will gain proficiency in the creation and interpretation of standard work charts and standard work combination sheets. That's good, because they should be revised often as new ideas for improvement are generated and as circumstances dictate, as shown below.

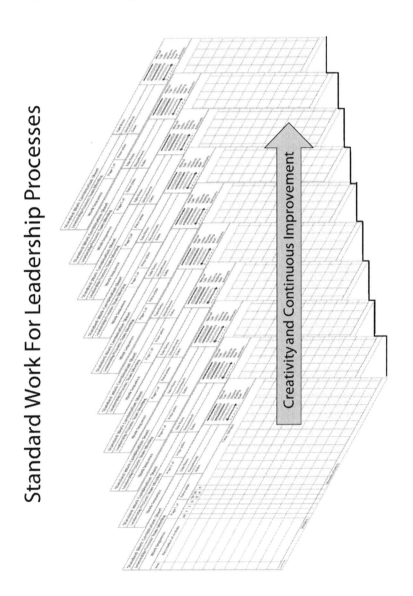

As a leader, your capacity for doing good work is limited by the standard working hours in a day: 8 hours. Most of the leadership processes are daily activities, as shown in bold, below. Therefore, leaders will cycle through many leadership processes each day.

1. **Leading and managing people**
2. Planning and budgeting
3. **Workload management**
4. **Decision-making**
5. **Problem recognition and response**
6. **Problem solving**
7. Management reviews (finance, operations, HR, etc.)
8. **Employee feedback and coaching**
9. **Team meetings**
10. **Asking questions, listening, and receiving feedback**
11. **Information sharing**
12. **Developing people**
13. Performance appraisal
14. **Walking around, "go see"**
15. **Stakeholder engagement (customers, suppliers, investors, communities)**

Leaders will also cycle through some leadership processes, such as 4, 5, 6, 10, 11, 12, and 14, several times a day. Leadership processes should be cycled in a sequence that makes sense for your organization, and in relation of the wants and needs of employees. They will view some leadership processes as more important to their ability to do good work than others. Consideration of their interests – consistent with the view of leadership as a service (LaaS) – will help eliminate employee dissatisfaction and strengthen trust between leaders and workers.

For example, my graduate students, who are full-time working professionals typically age 25 to 50, identified the leadership process errors shown in Chapter 2. I also ask them to identify the top leadership processes that their boss should standardize to improve quality and consistency. The results are shown on the following page.

The top six leadership processes they cite are:

1. Workload Management
2. Team Meetings
3. Developing People
4. Information Sharing
5. Problem-Solving
6. Walking Around, "Go See"

Why do employees pick these leadership processes? They pick these because they have the greatest impact on them personally. The error-filled performance by their leaders in these five processes is a source of immense frustration and dissatisfaction. This surely affects their ability to perform their work.

Most leaders, on the other hand, view these processes as too time-consuming and therefore either ignore them or perform them poorly. Indeed, in most organizations, these processes are very poor due complexity or other factors. Breaking down the process by using standard work charts and standard work combination sheets allows for complex processes to be simplified.

Additionally, these six leadership processes are plagued by delays, suggesting that leaders do not view delays as a problem – especially delays that do not affect them. They accept delays in these leadership processes as "just the way things are." These six leadership processes reflect the batch-and-queue way of thinking that is common among people in leadership positions.

Do not make the mistake of limiting standard work to the top six leadership processes, shown above, or select only those leadership processes that you like or seem to be easiest. These are examples meant to guide you towards your own answers. Think for yourself.

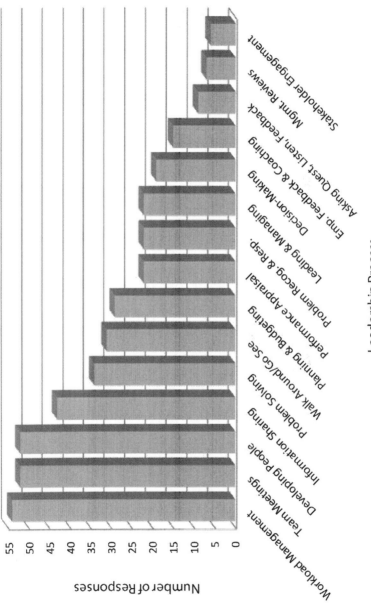

Leadership Process

Number of Responses

Another thing to consider is pay for performance. We have seen that leadership is an error-prone activity. Should leaders be highly compensated when they make many fundamental errors in their most basic of job responsibilities? Do organizations reward leaders who perform their leadership processes well, or do the rewards instead go mostly to the leaders that kick ass to get things done?

I ask my graduate students this question: If you were able to cut the pay of leaders for doing a bad job, what would be the basis for the pay cuts? Their collected response is:

- Sub-par leadership skills
- Not a role model
- Creates chaos
- Zero-sum (win-lose) leadership style
- Poor process management
- Does not care about employees
- Does not show respect or appreciation
- Selfish
- Does little actual work
- Delegates that which they should be doing
- Does not lead or improve
- Supports the status quo
- Does not motivate people
- Unclear expectations
- Too much confusion
- Does not influence people
- Not committed
- Ineffective
- Does not know the work people do
- Scary or intimidating leadership style
- Cannot be trusted
- No creativity or originality
- Micromanages the team
- Runs everything by the numbers

- Hands-off
- Afraid to make decisions
- Lacks common sense
- Limits employees' knowledge and abilities
- Withholds information
- Closed-minded

Because leaders are not directly involved in value-creating activities, they have a lot of time on their hands. That time is not used effectively, as is apparent from the above list. Leaders can easily make things worse for employees rather than better. The leader's focus should be on making things better for employees by continuously improving their own leadership processes.

Comprehending leadership as processes reveals all. The cover has been lifted, and what is exposed can no longer be defended as good quality leadership – despite one's personal history of success or press accounts of great leadership.

Leaders hope to instill a hunger for continuous improvement into workers. This is best accomplished though leading by example. Commitment to self-development, to improve your leadership processes, will inspire employees to improve their work processes. This, in turn, will improve the performance of teams, departments, and the company as a whole.

Questions For The Executive Team

Some important questions emerge from Chapter 6:

- Why do we think that continuous improvement methods and tools do not apply to our work?
- What has prevented us from using the same improvement methods and tools for our work as leaders?
- What will we have to do differently in the future to use improvement methods and tools for our leadership work?
- What new things do we have to study and learn?
- What new things do we need to practice every day?
- What does the Pareto chart look like for leadership processes in our organizations?
- Who will contact Bob Emiliani to get copies of the visual chart, standard work chart, and standard work combination sheet?

Discuss these questions as a senior management team. Use structured problem-solving processes to answer these questions and provide direction for improvement. Summarize the results of the discussion and problem-solving in two or three flip-chart pages, and post them on a wall for further thought and analysis.

Thoughts, Observations, and Actions To Take

Thoughts, Observations, and Actions To Take

7

Leadership Competency Models

For many years, organizations have used leadership competency models as a primary method for leadership development and to help create new organizational cultures. Competency models are generally accepted by human resources leaders and other senior managers as a useful way to help an organization meet its strategic objectives.

I twice participated in expensive, $12,000 per person, leadership development workshops in the mid- and late-1990s. These week-long evaluations by industrial psychologists featured a leadership competency model created by the company's HR consultant. The result of the evaluation of high potential individuals was the creation of individual development plans.

My first leadership development workshop was a worthwhile experience. However, most of my colleagues struggled to connect the leadership competency model to their day-to-day work activities. Leadership development and day-to-day work activities were seen as separate, but complimentary, because they used different language and had different objectives, goals, methods, and processes.

The lack of integration between hard-skills training and soft-skills training was a big problem. It meant that people had to make their own connections between their day-to-day work what the HR consultant was teaching them. Most were unsuccessful. As a result, most of the millions of dollars spent on developing a leadership competency model and on leadership development workshops was wasted. Organizations continue to struggle with this today. Their utility, overall, is questionable.

Traditional leadership competencies are generic, conceptual, harder to put into daily practice, and much easier to game. In addition, the definitions contained within traditional competency models are lengthy and subjective in their interpretation.

Speed Leadership closes the hard-skills, soft-skills gap without the need for expensive leadership competency models or workshops with industrial psychologists. Instead, it uses simple and practical methods improve leaders' skills and capabilities, to help organizations meet their strategic objectives. And, they are far more difficult to game or obfuscate.

But, to the extent that you find leadership competency models to be useful, the following pages show the relationship between the 15 leadership processes, competencies of progressive leaders, and 15 leadership competencies typically found in traditional HR competency models.

Please notice that the competencies of progressive leaders are far more specific, practical, and actionable than the leadership competencies found in traditional HR competency models. Likewise for the leadership processes in comparison to traditional HR competency models.

Also, notice that traditional leadership competencies (bottom row) do not result in progressive leader competencies (top row) that are needed for the rapidly changing times we now live in. However, the progressive leader competencies can result in the much sought-after traditional leadership competencies – while at the same time reducing leadership process errors.

If you choose to continue using leadership competency models, then you should follow the example shown in the matrices (but eliminate the bottom row). The general rules for ensuring that competency models are consistent with progressive leadership thinking and practice are as follows:

- Thoroughly integrate progressive leadership (top row) into leadership competency models.
- Keep all descriptions short.

- Cite specific actions, methods, tools, activities, or outcomes in descriptions. Outcomes should be non-financial.
- Simplify, always. Less is more because it results in better focus.
- Not more than one page.
- Use the same progressive leadership competency model for all levels of leadership, supervisor through CEO.

If there must be variation in competencies between the different levels, limit it to one critically important competency per level, and ensure that the competency does not contradict progressive leadership thinking and practice. All competencies must:

- Result in the reduction and elimination of leadership process errors.
- Move people from "Company Time" towards "Actual Time."
- Drive non-zero-sum thinking, behaviors, and outcomes.
- Promote the use of structured problem-solving methods (i.e. connect to the Scientific Method).
- Generate learning that is transferred to future leaders.

Relationship Between Progressive Leader Competencies, Leadership Processes, and Traditional Leadership Competencies

Progressive Leader Competencies → / Leadership Processes ↓	Participates in and leads process improvement activities to reduce costs, improve quality, and reduce lead-times. Develops ability to lead CI activities.	Listens, documents, and responds to employees' and customers' concerns. Prioritizes concerns based on employee or customer feedback and takes timely action.	Uses structured problem-solving (PDCA, A3 reports, root cause analysis) methods to quickly analyze problems and identify practical countermeasures.	Focuses on both process and results. Creates visual workplace and uses metrics to promote non-zero-sum behaviors and business outcomes.	Identifies motivation problems and develops simple plans to improve motivation.
1. Leading and managing people	X	X	X		X
2. Planning and budgeting	X				
3. Workload management	X	X		X	
4. Decision-making					
5. Problem recognition and response	X	X	X	X	X
6. Problem solving		X	X		X
7. Management reviews (finance, operations, human resources, etc.)	X		X	X	
8. Employee feedback and coaching		X		X	X
9. Team meetings	X				X
10. Asking questions, listening, and receiving feedback		X	X	X	X
11. Information sharing		X			X
12. Developing people	X	X	X	X	X
13. Performance appraisal					X
14. Walking around, "go see"		X			X
15. Stakeholder engagement (customer, supplier, investor, community)	X	X	X		X
Traditional Leadership Competencies	Business Acumen	Listening	Problem Solving	Managing and Measuring Work	Motivating Others

Relationship Between Progressive Leader Competencies, Leadership Processes, and Traditional Leadership Competencies

Leadership Processes \ Progressive Leader Competencies	Teaches and trains subordinates in improvement processes and structured problem-solving processes.	Identifies conflict, determines root causes of conflict, and eliminates conflict.	Focuses on the "vital few" activities to ensure that near-term commitments and mid-term strategy are achieved.	Seeks to understand sources and causes of variation to improve reliability and repeatability.	Seeks advice and information from others. Develops self as role model for others to follow.
1. Leading and managing people	X	X			X
2. Planning and budgeting			X	X	
3. Workload management			X		X
4. Decision-making	X		X		
5. Problem recognition and response		X	X	X	X
6. Problem solving	X	X	X	X	X
7. Management reviews (finance, operations, human resources, etc.)	X		X		
8. Employee feedback and coaching	X	X			X
9. Team meetings				X	
10. Asking questions, listening, and receiving feedback	X	X		X	X
11. Information sharing				X	
12. Developing people	X	X	X	X	X
13. Performance appraisal		X		X	X
14. Walking around, "go see"		X		X	
15. Stakeholder engagement (customer, supplier, investor, community)		X	X	X	
Traditional Leadership Competencies	Developing People	Conflict Management	Priority Setting	Dealing with Uncertainty	Self Awareness

Relationship Between Progressive Leader Competencies, Leadership Processes, and Traditional Leadership Competencies

Leadership Processes \ Progressive Leader Competencies	Understands decision-making traps and the different forms of illogical thinking. Tests beliefs and assumptions to improve decision-making. Seeks out contradictory opinions.	Persistently communicates vision and goals in relation to customer wants and needs. Reinforces customer as foundation of corporate purpose.	Understands the current state and works with team to rapidly achieve the future state. Improves responsiveness to changing conditions via daily improvement.	Creates and updates skills matrices. Promotes job rotation and cross-training. Coaches and mentors subordinates.	Leads by example. Able to do what is asked of others. A role model for consistency in words and actions.
1. Leading and managing people	X	X		X	X
2. Planning and budgeting	X		X	X	
3. Workload management			X	X	
4. Decision-making	X	X	X	X	X
5. Problem recognition and response	X				X
6. Problem solving	X	X	X	X	X
7. Management reviews (finance, operations, human resources, etc.)	X		X		
8. Employee feedback and coaching		X		X	X
9. Team meetings			X		
10. Asking questions, listening, and receiving feedback	X			X	X
11. Information sharing		X		X	X
12. Developing people	X	X	X	X	X
13. Performance appraisal					
14. Walking around, "go see"	X	X	X		X
15. Stakeholder engagement (customer, supplier, investor, community)	X	X	X		X
Traditional Leadership Competencies	Decision-Making	Communicates Vision and Purpose	Strategic Leadership	Assessing People	Influencing Others

Questions For The Executive Team

Some important questions emerge from Chapter 6:

- Why have we remained committed to competency models for so long, despite their lack of success?
- Do we look outside to see what is new and helpful, or are we too inwardly focused?
- Are competency models still useful? Should we not adopt Speed Leadership instead? What are the benefits? What are the risks?
- In making such decisions, how do we ensure our thinking and decision-making are free of bias, illogical thinking, and decision-making traps?
- What are the likely consequences of maintaining the status quo?
- In what ways can Speed Leadership better position us for the future?

Discuss these questions as a senior management team. Use structured problem-solving processes to answer these questions and provide direction for improvement. Summarize the results of the discussion and problem-solving in two or three flip-chart pages, and post them on a wall for further thought and analysis.

Thoughts, Observations, and Actions To Take

Thoughts, Observations, and Actions To Take

8

Closing Remarks

Leaders must be specialists in working with people, and they must develop levels of leadership performance that employees recognize as being that of a professional. They must be more adept at this than they are at working with numbers. Why? Because success with people leads to into success with processes, which, in turn, leads to success with numbers. Yet, many people who are great with numbers are promoted into leadership positions. Most are "leaders" by way of the position they hold in the organization, but not through their interactions with people. Employees expect that those who want to occupy leadership positions also want to lead. In the real world, there is always a gap between the two, but the gap is often much larger than it should be. An excellent way to close the gap is by accepting the existence of leadership process errors and learning how to improve leadership processes.

Speed Leadership presented a process view of leadership. This is a breakthrough in both our understanding of leadership as well as how to improve leadership skills and capabilities. It moves us past the traditional leadership competency model, organizational behavior, and organizational development approaches that have long been in existence but have yielded only modest results.

Comprehending leadership as processes makes it possible to easily identify errors. The specificity immediately suggests practical avenues for structured problem-solving and effective methods for improvement based upon the Scientific Method. This transforms leadership from art to science.

Each leader's performance, each team's performance, each department's performance, and the organization's performance will improve because the many simple, yet consequential errors that bedevil most organizations will be fewer and less frequent.

The easiest thing for leaders to do is deny that problems exist, or insist that problems have little or no impact on the organization because it has experienced years of success. Leaders may rationalize the hundreds of leadership process errors as insignificant. Yet, these errors have tangible effects on people, especially the employees who actually do the work. These mental, physical, and work-related effects are not free. They have costs and consequences that can only be denied by willfully ignoring reality. Doing so will almost surely be in conflict with your organization's code of conduct, ethics statements, or, at the very least, management rhetoric such as: "world-class," "performance culture," "excellence," and so on.

What looks like great performance and success must be viewed in relative terms. How much better could the organization be in fulfilling its purpose if leadership process errors were substantially reduced? It is not likely that reducing leadership process errors will result in unfavorable outcomes. You know from other improvement experiences that reducing errors and eliminating blocked information flows improves the work.

However, nothing is all upside. There will be some downsides that are obvious and some that are difficult to predict. One downside will be having to part ways with leaders who are unwilling to improve, as well as corporate psychopaths. The institutional heroes who thrive on chaos and who have been amply rewarded over the years for heroic deeds will not like the order and precision that comes with standard work. Voluntary separation is preferred, but some may have to be fired after if they fail to improve. In some cases, the person departing will be the CEO. Leadership changes will be necessary, despite their appearance of effectiveness, and it will feel as if there is tangible risk in doing so.

The more likely outcome is that leaders, most of whom want to improve, will recognize leadership process improvement as a great opportunity and take advantage of it. Most leaders do not like to lead by kicking ass. They know there is a better way, but are unsure of what to do given the poor record of past leadership development efforts – all of which were likely complex, expensive, and time consuming.

In contrast, leadership process improvement is not complex, expensive, or time-consuming. This little book has provided to you the bulk of the process errors that occur so that you do not have to pay a consultant to figure them out. You may want to pay a consultant to facilitate the creation of visuals or standard work, but that is not required. In addition, Speed Leadership allows you to eliminate expensive leadership development programs and traditional leadership competency models where it makes sense to do so.

The behavioral and technical capabilities that leaders develop by improving leadership processes (e.g. visuals and standard work) are likely similar to other improvement activities going on throughout the organization. Leaders are learning new things that are highly relevant to their job. This will result in broad alignment across the organization with respect to understanding and improving processes.

Speed Leadership will have great impact among leaders who understand it as a solution for information flow problems in organizations, and, ultimately, a method for improving human health in organizations.

Good luck!

Thoughts, Observations, and Actions To Take

Thoughts, Observations, and Actions To Take

Acknowledgements

I wish to thank the graduate students/working professionals in my Innovative Leadership course (TM 572) who produced many of leadership process errors shown in Chapter 2; the list of mental, physical, work, and other effects presented in Chapter 3; for inspiring three of the four leadership process visuals; and the pay-cut responses presented at the end of Chapter 6.

About the Author

M.L. "Bob" Emiliani is a professor in the School of Engineering, Science, and Technology at Connecticut State University in New Britain, Conn., where he teaches a course on progressive leadership, a unique course that analyzes failures in management decision-making, as well as other courses.

Bob holds a Bachelor of Science degree in mechanical engineering from the University of Miami, a Master's degree in chemical engineering from the University of Rhode Island, and a Ph.D. degree in Engineering from Brown University.

He worked in the consumer products and aerospace industries for 15 years, beginning as a materials engineer. He has held management positions in engineering, manufacturing, and supply chain management, and had responsibility for continuous improvement in manufacturing and supply chains at Pratt & Whitney.

Bob joined academia in September 1999 at Rensselaer Polytechnic Institute (Hartford, Connecticut campus) and worked there until 2004. He joined Connecticut State University in 2005. While in academia, he developed a new teaching pedagogy and led activities to continuously improve master's degree programs.

Emiliani has authored or co-authored more than 16 books, four book chapters, over 45 peer-reviewed papers He has received six awards for writing.

Please visit www.bobemiliani.com

Made in the USA
Middletown, DE
21 September 2018